What Is a Commons?

Any place in which people assemble,
indoors or outdoors,
irrespective of the duration of its occupancy,
can be considered a potential commons.

Sharing in the envisioning of
what a supportive and uplifting meeting place might be
can awaken people's sense of being in community.
It can reawaken the commons.

People can stake their claim on a commons
through instant transformation of spaces,
barnraising and animating temporary settings for special occasions,
or building lasting neighborhood and community garden commons.

BUILDING COMMONS AND COMMUNITY

KARL LINN

New Village Press
Oakland, California

A good faith effort has been made to obtain necessary permissions and proper credits for all photographs in this book. Please contact the publisher regarding any omissions or corrections; the publisher will include revised credits in all future editions.

Published by New Village Press
P.O. Box 3049, Oakland, CA 94609
Orders: (510) 420-1361; press@newvillage.net
www.newvillagepress.net

New Village Press is a public-benefit, not-for-profit publishing venture of Architects/Designers/Planners for Social Responsibility. www.adpsr.org

Interior book design by Diana Young
Printed and bound in China.

Library of Congress Cataloging-in-Publication Data

Linn, Karl.
  Building commons and community / by Karl Linn.
    p. cm.
  Summary: "Documents 44 years of the late Karl Linn's work creating neighborhood commons, such as community gardens, playgrounds and parks. Includes a dozen photographically-illustrated case studies. Offers practical advice on engaging professionals with local populations in collaborative community development"-- Provided by publisher.
  Includes index.
  ISBN 978-0-9766054-7-8 (hardcover : alk. paper)
  1. Commons--United States. 2. Commons--United States--Case studies. 3. Community development-- United States--Case studies. 4. Community life--United States. I. Title.
HD1289.U6L56 2007
333.2--dc22
                                2007016286

TABLE OF CONTENTS

FOREWORD

It's a Monday morning in late August and the first time I've walked here without him. The fanciful ironwork of the Sunflower Gate, crispy with rust, is beautiful as ever, a good welcome to the Peralta Community Garden and the Northside Garden, which extends beyond it where the long lot narrows along the tracks. Entering, I pause to take in the scene. With no Karl at my side hurrying me along to the next new feature or explaining his latest strategy to recruit support, I can be still now and take my time.

The early fog is beginning to lift. The sun breaking through ignites warmth in my bones and color in the planting beds. All hues of reds and yellows flame out from poppies, marigolds, ripe tomatoes. The garden bursts with vitality, each planting bed a fountain of fertility to make your mouth water and your hands hanker to reach out and pick. This luxuriance surprises me, for I'd grown accustomed to seeing the garden half-built. The beds were barely sketched out before we began coming

for ritual events, like the gathering Karl called, early on, for dialogue between Muslims and Jews.

I met Karl a quarter-century ago amidst citizen actions against the nuclear arms race. In the early 1980s Reagan policies made nuclear war an ever-closer possibility. Karl had co-founded Architects/ Designers/Planners for Social Responsibility and spoke enthusiastically about the role his professional colleagues could play in building a culture capable of peace.

Like many of our colleagues in the anti-nuclear movement, Karl could have devoted himself ongoingly to organizational work on the national and global scene. But he couldn't keep his hands out of the soil or his mind off neighborhoods. His vision of building commons and community, in the most immediate, practical fashion, drew him like a magnet.

I count three kinds of bees humming amidst the blossoms, burrowing into sweet peas, snapdragons, lavender. White butterflies flicker like minutes through the climbing pole beans. Wheelbarrows lean against the tool shed, beside cuttings and weeds piled for compost from the weekend's work. In the open circle made by the curving, tiled bench at the garden's center, a woman is doing tai chi. Almost my age and a lot spryer, she opens her arms in a slow, wide arc, revolves on one foot, and lifts her face to the sun.

Maybe this is how you stop nuclear war.

You make a place that belongs to everyone. A place where life is beautiful and strong. A place where you claim your right to nourish and be nourished.

Or maybe, if nuclear war in its distant and multiplying guises cannot be stopped, to survive it. And, in equal measure, to prepare for and survive other catastrophes we hadn't imagined a quarter-century ago. Oil depletion and collapsed supplylines of food. Climate change and hunger from drought and flooding. Genetic modification of seeds, eroding health as more and more crops are contaminated.

These crises awaken us to the imperative for collective action. They summon us to the essential adventure of our time: the shift to a life-sustaining society. Comparable in magnitude to the agricultural and industrial revolutions, this third one is occurring now, in our time. Many are calling it, quite simply, the Great Turning.

These commons brought forth by Karl are a manifestation of the Great Turning.

Spaced amidst the beds and along the perimeters are works of art, in stone, metal, wood, ceramic.

Perusing a six-foot Escher-like construction of steel rebar, I see that it is entitled "Homage to Piranesi." The artist's words on a clay plaque identify Piranesi as a sixteenth-century Venetian printmaker, whose "work helps us widen our visual conception while challenging our artistic imagination… (Thus conveying) both specific precision and unseen reality."

Well, the unseen reality I'm sensing here feels like hope. It's the promise that lies in human hearts and hands.

"Gardens and art share some similar purposes—they nourish us and sustain us," reads another clay plaque, where arching branches shade two ancient, bright-green chairs. "They help us survive difficult times, and bring us the deepest and simplest joys."

When I finally allow myself to leave, after contemplating every plot and piece of art, I stand by the entrance for one last quiet moment. Ah, here's a plaque I haven't read yet. "This sunflower gate," writes Amy Blackstone who made it, "marks the threshold, not only where the city sidewalk leaves off and the earth with all her wild mysteries beckons us forth, but the very place where someone once stood looking at a dusty, littered vacant lot dreaming of a garden where people, art, beauty could flourish and nourish the self as much as the fruits and vegetables of one's own labor. Welcome to that dream!"

Welcome to this book. May it kindle many more such dreams.

Joanna Macy

INTRODUCTION

We live in a high-pressure, competitive society, with increasing concerns about security. Residents of cities and suburbs deeply miss meaningful human contact and the presence of a supportive community. The process of creating commons can provide that contact and support.

Commons are gathering spaces—indoor or outdoor—that people have personalized to meet the needs of their community. They are places where neighborhood residents young and old can gather face-to-face, to relax, talk, and enjoy each other's company. In commons, people also assemble to celebrate special occasions and debate issues that affect their lives.

Our physical surroundings have a deep impact on our experience of life. We are inspired by a tree-lined city block, an aesthetically pleasing building, a work of public art. Drab surroundings, by contrast, leave us feeling depressed. In impersonal, institutional settings, we feel alienated and isolated. Such regimented settings foster passivity. An environment that lacks the imprint of personal or communal art or craftsmanship does not encourage participation and creative expression.

People need to build shared spaces that enliven their senses, express their visions, and strengthen their connection to the natural world. When neighbors participate in envisioning, building, and using a shared communal space, they simultaneously build relationships with one another. In thriving, healthy communities the visions and creativity of all community members are reflected in their immediate physical surroundings.

The photo essays in this book represent over forty years of creating such shared spaces. In community after community, many of them not documented here, I worked alongside neighborhood residents to develop communal gathering places that would meet the needs of the people living nearby. We engaged children, teens, women, and men in the design process. We found ways to cooperate with city agencies and social service agencies, who made available large-scale machinery and resources. We solicited the advice of design professionals and others, who willingly gave of their time and expertise to work with neighborhood residents.

My intention is to provide a resource for anyone interested in using the physical environment to build community—neighborhood residents, community organizers, artists, landscape architects, architects and planners, social and environmental activists, people of faith, educators, students, and many others. The final chapter on "Foundations of Commons Building" gives practical guidelines on the process of creating commons.

Origins

I spent my childhood in Germany, attuned to the wonders of nature on my mother's fruit tree farm, which was also an accredited training center for gardeners and offered horticultural therapy. During the early 1930s, however, as the only Jewish child in our small village, I experienced racial discrimination. When I was eleven, our family was displaced, fleeing Germany to escape Nazi persecution.

As a young teenager in Palestine, I had to leave school and support my parents by operating a small farm. Later I completed a program at an agricultural school and went on to serve an apprenticeship in landscape architecture. With friends from the Scouting movement I co-founded a kibbutz. The egalitarian spirit, sense of common purpose, and closeness to the land inspired me. Yet community on the kibbutz was far from complete since it excluded Arabs from membership. When illness forced me to leave the kibbutz, I developed a gardening program in an elementary school in Tel Aviv. Having experienced racism and persecution, I had a deep desire to study human nature. I underwent psychoanalysis and body-oriented therapy to heal my own traumas. To become a therapist I earned degrees in psychology in Switzerland and engaged in a training analysis. Moving to the United States, I practiced child psychoanalysis and cofounded a

school for emotionally disturbed children. Learning about human nature and gaining insight into mental health guided my aspiration to contribute to the building of a multicultural, cooperative, and nonviolent society.

Becoming aware of the intricately interwoven connection between body and mind, I realized that in order to continue responsibly in my therapeutic work, I needed to study medicine, but, as it turned out, that was not a good match for me. At the same time, as a result of my inner work, I felt a growing desire to express myself creatively, particularly in giving form to open spaces.

Since nature had always been a source of sanity and inspiration, I decided to give up my work in psychology in 1951 and re-enter landscape architecture, which I began to think of as a healing profession. Within natural settings, especially in the presence of powerful, majestic landscapes, we experience our humanness more fully. Our petty grievances seem insignificant under the dome of stars. As we inhale the cool air of towering forests, we stop clenching our teeth and start to relax. Experiencing the flow of our protoplasm resonating with the surging of the ocean, we feel humble and ennobled—part of a large and magnificent universe. Among the design professions, landscape architecture concerns itself with a unique blend of nature and civilization, art and science, heart and intellect.

I experienced gratifying success as a landscape architect during the 1950s, designing many residential landscapes for wealthy clients on the eastern sea-

Bringing people together in their shared environments became my life's calling.

board. Yet the very prosperity of my clients became a source of discontent: I was now creating primarily landscapes of affluence. When I reviewed my portfolio of landscapes I had created, I realized to my consternation that they were devoid of people. In only one photo did a small girl appear, playing in a sandbox. At that time, spaces designed by architects and landscape architects were perceived more as static sculptures than as arenas for living.

The suburbs, where I did most of my work, were designed around the automobile, often with no sidewalks. They looked like "green deserts," devoid of places to socialize, and consequently devoid of people. I observed that the women, who lived in those houses during the day without male support, were left alone to raise their children. In many suburbs there were no benches or common areas for socializing or promoting neighborliness, and children lacked easily accessible public play areas. Families were isolated from one another by fences or hedges. I empathized deeply with the plight of nuclear families. The subdivisions where I worked were planned so that male breadwinners, who faced tremendous social and mental pressures at work, could relax at night and on weekends in the solitary peacefulness of their homes and landscapes. I realized that professional designers could democratize the practice of architecture and landscape architecture by introducing participatory design processes that would engage women, children, and teenagers. Bringing people together in their shared environments became my life's calling.

To give deeper meaning and social relevance to my work, I took a teaching position at the University of Pennsylvania Department of Landscape Architecture in 1959. The search for models of a more livable neighborhood envi-

ronment led me to Radburn, a subdivision in Fairlawn, New Jersey, designed by Clarence Stein in 1928. There I found pedestrian and vehicular traffic separated through overpasses and was delighted to see children playing in utter safety. Radburn also augmented people's private yards with a network of pedestrian pathways leading to expanses of common areas where various-sized groups of people milled about. The network of "commons," easily accessible to people of all ages, improved the quality of their lives significantly.

The absence of viable community life in the suburbs, caused by the lack of available and easily accessible open spaces, was voiced succinctly by my friend Marilyn Guerra in a letter to me on February 20, 1963, after I had created neighborhood commons in Philadelphia and Washington:

> Rockville [Maryland] has no slums, and very few substandard dwellings. Our families share in the prosperity of Montgomery County, as a whole. Our city has a very adequate program of parkland acquisition and improvement to meet the active recreational needs of our growing population. The problem, then, is the lack of intimate, casual meeting grounds within our gridiron-style housing developments. There is no destination for young mothers pushing strollers, no place for husbands to congregate on summer evenings. While most neighborhoods are physically small enough to be thought of as units, these units have no focal point, and consequently no identity to those who live there.

I learned from my mentor Lawrence K. Frank, a social innovator who was a visiting lecturer at the university, that rural extended families had provided much more emotional and physical support than the nuclear families that people formed when they moved into the cities. Larry and his family were creating a new kind of extended family, sharing a communal household with Margaret Mead and Gregory Bateson and their daughter, Mary Catherine.

Aspiring to give greater social relevance to landscape architecture, I developed a Community Design-and-Build Service Program in Landscape Architecture that introduced my students to low-income inner-city neighborhoods, exploring ways that we could serve those who could not afford professional design services. These inner-city neighborhoods were occupied mainly by single-mother, people-of-color families who, even more than the isolated women living in the suburbs, needed the support that extended-family living could provide. Since parks and playgrounds in these neighborhoods were not easily accessible, children played on sidewalks and streets amid hazardous traffic. Neighbors badly needed safe and accessible open spaces in residential blocks that could serve as extensions of home territory.

Barnraising Commons

As my graduate students and I visited low-income communities in North Philadelphia, we saw many vacant lots filled with weeds, garbage, and dilapidated buildings that had been subjected to arson or neglect. We envisioned some of them becoming easily accessible, safe open spaces, managed by local residents, that would combine the functions of sitting areas, neighborhood parks, playgrounds, and community gardens. We called these spaces "neighborhood commons."

Hoping that some of the many unemployed men in these neighborhoods and some of the teenagers who hung around on street corners would join the women and children in building the commons, we imagined that the experience of interdependence would generate a growing sense of extended family living based not on blood relationship but on growing friendship, mutual aid, and intergenerational support. Ideally the successful experience of creating neighborhood commons, and sharing their accessible, intimate spaces, would inspire residents to participate actively in their neighborhood block community, which is the bedrock of grassroots democracy.

I realized that this would be an adaptation of the old American tradition of "barnraising" to an urban setting. Just as farmers used to pool their efforts in the process of constructing a barn, these inner-city dwellers would be working together to build shared spaces, together achieving what each could not do alone. In the United States the image of barnraising may be a painful one for Native Americans, who were purged from the land on which European immigrants built their barns, and for African Americans, who toiled as slaves constructing the edifices of their masters. But collective work celebrations are practiced by indigenous people the world over.

To make the construction of neighborhood commons by low-income neighborhood residents

All the commons projects I participated in were informed by the principles of grassroots democracy, communal creativity, and wise use of readily available materials.

economically feasible, we engaged in creative recycling of salvageable building material from nearby urban renewal demolition sites. Using historic building material, such as worn bricks, flagstones, and marble steps, we integrated the newly constructed neighborhood commons into the physical fabric and aesthetic of the neighborhood, in a way that new construction material never could.

Depending on people's needs and the resources available—of labor, motivation, building materials, and money—we created three types of commons: lasting neighborhood gathering places; instant commons, where people transform a space in a matter of minutes; and temporary commons, where people come together for a number of days or weeks to transform a gathering place for a special occasion or conference. Each type of commons presents its own creative challenges, which the people involved must work together to solve. In the process, individual creativity is unleashed and impersonal, drab public spaces are transformed into places of beauty.

The early neighborhood commons projects brought together diverse participants: residents of inner cities, volunteer professionals, members of social service and religious organizations, environmental and social justice activists, and young people enrolled in training and employment programs. Engaging people in barnraising commons fosters personal growth, heightens social awareness, and nurtures a sense of community. Over the years, we found ways to encourage more people to participate in creating commons and developed methods for resolving conflicts and maintaining open communication, allowing both ideas and emotions to be expressed. These are the paths to deeper mutual understanding and stronger bonds among diverse members of a

community. All the commons projects I participated in were informed by the principles of grassroots democracy, communal creativity, and wise use of readily available materials.

Since the days of the early commons I revisited the projects in which I had participated at least once each decade. Some of the projects from the 1960s and 1970s that were envisioned to be lasting commons were preserved and restored; others no longer exist, having fallen prey to economic pressures for construction of affordable housing. One was displaced by the expansion of a settlement house, another by an affordable senior-citizen apartment building surrounded by a formidable fence. Three were encaged by tall fences to improve security in residential neighborhoods plagued by asocial activities.

A major problem with the early neighborhood commons was that they featured very little vegetation. Since no one needed to visit them regularly to care for the plants, the commons were not well-maintained. In the 1990s, while living in California, I began to work with community gardeners who are not only eager to grow fresh produce close to home, but also eager to socialize. Unfortunately many community gardens are devoid of sociability settings. Combining community gardens with neighborhood commons became the most successful strategy I found for building lasting, cared-for neighborhood commons.

In the process of constructing each commons, neighbors came to know one another more deeply and conceived strategies for dealing with the inevitable conflicts that arise when people work closely together. They developed participatory processes that drew more members of the community into the creative process and broadened the base of neighborhood involvement.

PHOTO ESSAYS OF COMMONS PROJECTS

LOUISE DUNLAP

A CLUSTER OF NEIGHBORHOOD COMMONS

CREATING COMMUNITY BY BUILDING AND USING COMMONS

In community garden commons the cultivation of plants predominates. Commons within lasting, cared-for community gardens are also enduring and well-maintained. The pleasure gardeners derive from their personal plots inspires them to take on communal responsibilities and collaborate with other gardeners in caring for common spaces. Working together, they grow community along with plants.

National statistics indicate that although the first priority of community gardeners is to grow fresh produce close to home, they also want to use the garden for socializing with one another and with family and friends. Incorporating shaded areas, benches, and tables among the planting beds transforms community gardens into viable neighborhood meeting places. Works of art, colorful native plants, and eco-friendly technologies enrich the gardens, making them more vibrant and beautiful, instilling pride, and inspiring care.

The spirit of the commons cannot be reawakened overnight. Accustomed to a competitive society and isolated nuclear families, people often feel burdened when they take on communal responsibility. Community garden commons provide a training ground to cultivate interaction based on collaboration and mutual support.

In the early neighborhood commons, we focused more on physical construction than on vegetation. Without many plants, the commons did not require daily maintenance, yet they suffered from the wear and tear of intensive use. After the exhausting work of creating the commons, especially large commons in low-income areas, neighbors hoped municipal recreation departments would provide upkeep and repairs. Unfortunately, these agencies refused to maintain open spaces that they had not built themselves.

Securing land for community gardens, under the administration of grassroots communities, helps to counter the worldwide privatizing of natural resources—the ongoing enclosure of the commons. Although the size of each commons is small, reclaiming a network of commons in residential neighborhoods throughout the city—ideally one lot per block—can empower grassroots communities and contribute to the democratization of society.

Members of Berkeley's Community Gardening Collaborative met in the commons to celebrate the award of a grant from the Healthy Cities Program.

Karl Linn Community Garden Commons

A Resource for the Community

Berkeley, California, 1993

July 25, 1993 is a day I'll never forget. As I walked with my wife, Nicole, down Hopkins Street, near my home in north Berkeley, I noticed a very large group of people congregating in a small run-down community garden. As I approached, people cheered. Together, they had organized a belated surprise party for my 70th birthday. The expression of friendship and acknowledgment by so many of my friends and colleagues, many of whom I hadn't seen in years, overwhelmed me.

But how had everyone been discovered and contacted? I soon learned that a few friends had come up with the idea of dedicating an open space in my name and had settled on this unnamed community garden. They had brought the proposal to Berkeley's Parks and Recreation Commission, who had asked them to come back with approval from neighbors. So they went knocking on doors in the area to introduce the idea.

Some neighborhood residents expressed concern about a community garden that glorified the name of one individual, but my friends reassured them when they explained that I had devoted my life to community participation. With sufficient approval from neighbors and letters of recommendations from respected community leaders, the Commission approved the idea. During six months of planning, the event somehow remained a secret to me.

My friends John and Michelle Thelen Steere and Elan Shapiro collaborated with my wife and others to stage a very moving event. First a Welcoming Circle created a context for the program. After a ritual to create sacred space, Mayor Loni Hancock and city councilwoman Linda Maio read a proclamation and unveiled a sign carved by my stepdaughter, Nomi Wanag. Old friends and colleagues expressed their appreciation for my work, and the event concluded with a Snake Dance through the garden and up a few blocks to Cedar-Rose Park for a potluck picnic and birthday celebration with musical performances and sing-along.

Sign carved by Karl's stepdaughter, Nomi Wanag

Friends and colleagues took turns addressing the gathering.

I remember most vividly the song my wife composed, "Places of Peace," which she played on a keyboard in the garden, while everyone joined in singing:

Places of peace
Gardens of green
Standing together, we're growing
Visions of wholeness coming.

Friendship can be a reality
Harmony can be for you and for me, Oh!

Places of peace
Gardens of green
Standing together, we're growing.

My response to the statements and good wishes of my friends surprised me:

Since places are usually dedicated as memorials, and since this garden will outlive me, I am confronted with issues of life and death. Today's dedication reminds me of another time in my life when I survived, escaping from Nazi persecution. That made me experience life thereafter as a second chance. It motivated me to devote my life to service, to the building of a non-totalitarian society. I am sure that all the expressions of love and goodwill, which are not easy for me to assimilate, will add many years to my life.

Across the street, landscape architecture professor Linda Jewell viewed the overgrown and unsightly garden daily through a large window in her living room. Throughout the summer, she and I met several times to explore alternative designs to counter this visual assault. Though we hadn't the slightest idea where we would obtain the resources to implement our ideas, we wanted to give the garden redesign a chance.

In early September, Linda had to go back to teaching and could no longer work on the project. Instead, she asked if I thought she should offer a class that would enable the students to participate in the redesign and construction of the garden. The idea delighted me, as a class would offer a rare opportunity for students to build a project of their own design.

The garden before the dedication

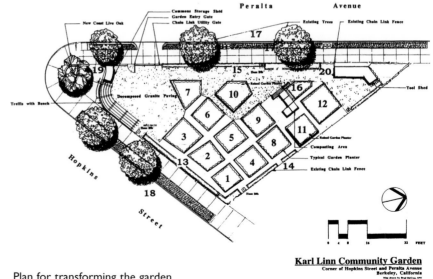

Plan for transforming the garden

19

Finished arbor-trellis with curved bench

Janice Sandeen at the UC Berkeley woodshop

The class was composed of nine graduate students who met weekly with Linda, landscape contractor Neil Collier who also lived in the neighborhood, garden coordinator Herb Weber, wood sculptor Scott Constable, and me. At times neighbors would also join us. On one occasion we met with Dave Faison, owner of Into the Woods, a huge recycled lumber depot in Petaluma, who showed us samples of his lumber. We also recruited Janice Sandeen, a wood sculptor who chaired the Wood Department at the California College of Arts and Crafts, to assist Scott, who remained eager to participate as a volunteer in designing and constructing the wooden structures.

After neighbors reviewed various revisions of the sketches and plans, we submitted the designs to Berkeley's Department of Parks and Waterfront for approval. The students constructed an artfully executed model of the commons, which helped neighbors visualize the proposal and offer constructive suggestions. After numerous changes specified by the Department of Public Works (DPW) engineer, we finally obtained building and zoning permits.

Fortuitously, at that time the City of Berkeley needed to spend $1.5 million of accrued profits from its Public Employee Retirement Service Fund (PERS) on park improvements. Herb Weber encouraged us to apply for funding and use it to add a commons, a toolshed, and wheelchair-accessible pathways, which would make the garden a more significant community resource.

Making the commons a public amenity was essential for receiving municipal funding. Critics asserted that a fence and locked gate proved that the community garden commons was not a public resource. I argued that it was a social equity issue: low-income community gardeners, who rely on the produce from their plots, deserve the same security enjoyed by affluent homeowners. Herb and I started the HopPer Commons Association to interface with the general public, taking the name from our intersection, Hopkins Street and Peralta Avenue.

We received a grant of $10,000, more than half our request, which we used to purchase building materials. Volunteer labor made the project feasible, and Neil Collier, who had a contractor's license, offered to receive the money and procure project materials at contractor's prices.

AmeriCorps Teams

Much of the manual labor far exceeded the capability of garden plot holders and neighbors, so we contacted several organizations that recruit volunteers. Earlier in the year, I had given a talk to 150 AmeriCorps volunteers as part of their service-learning program. Inspired by my talk about self-help construction of neighborhood commons, they responded enthusiastically when I requested a team to work on the garden.

Working with them gave continuity to my efforts during the early 1960s when I founded the Neighborhood Renewal Corps of Philadelphia and the Neighborhood Commons Nonprofit Corporation of Washington, DC. These organizations, which channeled the skills and energy of students and volunteer professionals into community design service for underserved inner-city residents, became models for the development of a national service corps, known for many years as VISTA and more recently as AmeriCorps.

The AmeriCorps team and UC Berkeley students worked hard to remove invasive fennel and to excavate planting beds along the edge of the garden. AmeriCorps team members also created wheelchair-accessible pathways, excavating and filling them with four inches of decomposed granite (DG), which they framed with planks and separated from the soil with a screen. In addition, they constructed raised beds

The toolshed was built from recycled material, its sliding doors purchased from a salvage yard. Our master craftsperson, wood sculptor Scott Constable, was assisted by students. Some of the knot holes in the lumber were filled in with colored glass, adding a unique dimension to the shed. The network of wheelchair accessible pathways extended to create a small courtyard with benches in front of the toolshed.

for people with injured backs and those in wheelchairs. They also restored the frames of the existing beds with redwood planks supplied by Berkeley's Department of Public Works and aligned the beds so that wheelbarrows could maneuver easily between them.

Salvaged Materials

We built all the wood structures from salvaged lumber. The ten-by-ten-inch support beams of the cantilevered arbor came from an eleven-mile-long train trestle bridge, deconstructed and dismantled from across the Great Salt Lake in Utah. Luckily, we also found a very large slab of salvaged cypress that allowed us to make the curved bench from one con-

tinuous piece of wood. Though the students were unable to finish the project within the limits of their academic semester, they got enormous satisfaction from participating in this construction.

Besides the ecological benefits of using salvaged wood for construction, its high quality and visual character provided an unexpected aesthetic reward. As Linda Jewell remarked, "The design grows out of the uniqueness of the piece of material itself."

Initially the city hesitated to approve the use of salvaged materials in an outdoor structure because of the risk of insect infestation. The building team responded by raising the bases of the posts higher off the ground and by coating the wood

Gardeners
tend their plots.

The bench and water
fountain outside the
garden function as a
mini-commons.

with generous amounts of linseed oil to prevent water rot.
Eventually, city officials were convinced of the wood's
integrity and now require that only salvaged or certified
sustainably harvested redwood be used on city landscape
projects.

Since the garden borders Berkeley's Ohlone
Greenway, we also created an inviting spot for cyclists and
hikers to take a break. We pulled back the garden boundary and created a curved bench outside the arbor, using a
single, very wide piece of wood. A live oak tree, donated
by Neil Collier's firm, Live Oak Landscapes, shaded the
bench. Local sculptor Martin Metal crafted an attractive
drinking fountain.

The plot holders, inspired by the transformation of
the space, became more enthusiastic about tending their
beds, and the garden flourished.

Children from nearby Ala Costa School with their teacher work in the garden.

Members of the East Bay Palestinian-Jewish Dialogue Group gather for
the ceremonial planting of a peace pole in the Peralta Garden.

Peralta and Northside Community Art Garden Commons
Reclaiming Land for Commons, Art, and Eco-friendly Technology

Berkeley, California, Fall 1996

Many of the prospective gardeners on the Karl Linn Community Garden waiting list were landless apartment dwellers eager to have a plot, so I was eager to develop the empty lot across the street as an additional community garden. I corresponded with members of BART's board of directors and real estate division director, Desha Hill, and enlisted the aid of our local City Councilmember Linda Maio. Linda organized the first meeting of neighbors interested in creating the two community gardens and gave us good news. She had a lease signed by BART and the City of Berkeley, and she had obtained ten thousand dollars from the city council as seed money for construction of the garden.

Local resident Lisa Chow made an impassioned plea to have artists and teenagers participate in the development of the garden, and the group agreed that the gardens should be designed as works of art. Heightening their aesthetic appeal would draw people from the larger community. As artist Fran Segal pointed out, infusing the community gardens with works of beauty would also "nurture the human spirit, offering a refuge from our frantic daily urban existence." Disability activist Philip Chavez urged that the gardens have generous pathways for wheelchair accessibility, like the ones made of compacted, sandlike decomposed granite (DG) in the Karl Linn Community Garden across the street.

The Peralta Community Garden sign was created by Remi Rubel, who is well known for her creative use of salvaged materials, including something she calls "roadkill metal." Her collaborator was Mani Simmons, a teenage artist.

I have an innate sense of seeing beauty in stuff other people consider garbage and pass by. I've had it since I was a kid. There's so much waste. We're throwing away a lot that is completely reusable. We need to change and see waste as a resource, not garbage.

—Remi Rubel

To maintain good relations and assure that noise from the construction phase not come as a surprise, we visited neighbors who had not come to the meetings, especially those whose properties abutted the gardens. We scheduled work parties to clear the site and announced them in the neighborhood. Volunteers raked up gravel remaining from the BART tunnel construction and hauled it to the area reserved for access by repair equipment. Others collected debris, such as broken bottles, metal pieces, and chunks of cement, and hauled it to the dump. Retired mechanic Ray Winnie offered his auger to drill into our compacted soil to take samples for testing, and we were overjoyed when lab results showed no pollution and a high mineral content.

Most of the gardeners lived in affordable-housing apartment buildings nearby. They came from different cultural backgrounds and represent several generations. "Grandpa," an expert gardener and recent immigrant from China, who didn't speak a word of English, drew on his agricultural experience to create a flourishing garden. One of our African-American gardeners, usually accompanied by his grandson, enthusiastically applied his extensive knowledge of making compost to the garden. The newly elected young Korean garden coordinator, who had no prior contact with neighbors, delighted in new friendships with her fellow gardeners. She shared seeds her mother had recently sent her for a Korean delicacy with another young Korean woman. Two middle-aged women, who had been

I wanted this gate to celebrate the whimsy of such a radical idea as turning an abandoned lot into a garden, so I let the wayward sunflowers lead the project while soon insects, lizards, ravens, great blue herons and rabbits began cheering from the sidelines. As I worked, the challenge of connecting each leaf, bloom, bug, and animal (lest the whole thing fall in jigsaw pieces to the ground) became a lovely metaphor for how interconnected and interdependent we all are on one another and the planet for our health and happiness.

This Sunflower Gate marks the threshold—not only where the city sidewalk leaves off and the earth with all her wild mysteries beckons us forth but the very place where Karl Linn once stood looking at a dusty, littered vacant lot dreaming of a garden where people, art, and beauty could flourish and nourish the Self as much as the fruits and vegetables of one's own labor.

Welcome to that dream!

—statement by sculptor Amy Blackstone, who created the gate at her own expense and donated it to the garden

Amy at work in her studio

© EDWARD CALDWELL

The "Sunflower Gate" is the main entrance to the Peralta Community Garden.

27

For the dedication of the Peralta and Northside Community Art Gardens, we installed "Creek Banners" along the main pedestrian pathway to the center of the Peralta Commons. The banners, provided by John Steere and the East Bay Citizens for Creek Restoration, depict plants and animals that live in and around local streams and are designed to create a symbolic riparian (creekside vegetation) zone. Groups of children and adults had painted them as a community art project.

high school pals thirty-five years earlier, were delighted to find themselves occupying adjacent plots. We all marveled at how the blind partner of another gardener participated actively in the preparation and planting of vegetables.

In October 1997 we decided to stage a fall harvest celebration dedicating the Peralta and Northside Community Gardens, celebrating our accomplishments, and acknowledging all the hard work by volunteers. Local artists provided a festive setting when they created temporary art installations for the event. The program included music, poetry, and song that honored the tremendous collaborative efforts to create the gardens and the hopes they generated. The garden coordinators and design and construction team leaders spoke briefly before the mayor, BART director, and our city councilwoman officially dedicated the gardens.

As part of a greening ceremony and procession through the banner-lined pathways conducted by choreographer Carla DeSola, participants ceremonially cast handfuls of rock dust on the planting beds to stimulate the growth of microorganisms, regenerate productive soil, and produce lush plant growth. Closing statements envisioning the future were followed by a potluck and socializing.

A Tai Chi class in the Peralta Garden Commons

Bringing offerings to a neighborhood potluck held in the Commons

Farmers' Market manager and poet Kirk Lumpkin and his wife, Hannah Field, celebrated their wedding in the Peralta Garden Commons. Later Kirk staged poetry events in the commons.

While community gardeners are primarily interested in growing crops and flowers in their own individual planting beds, they become members of a larger community in the garden. Their participation in construction, maintenance, and administration is entirely voluntary. Unlike regular employment situations, in which workers may be forced to swallow their pride and tolerate humiliation and indignities to avoid jeopardizing their paychecks, the participation of community gardeners requires that their involvement be enjoyable.

It is easy to inadvertently step on the toes of a fellow gardener, especially when the work is challenging and physically exhausting. Misunderstandings, hurts, resentments, and anger can waste much energy. To maintain their good spirits, volunteers need opportunities to air repressed negative emotions and resolve conflicts. Unhappy volunteers will simply walk off the project. As we struggle with the scars of our upbringing, we are often unaware of our own problems, ego, and power issues, so collaborative efforts provide opportunities for growth, healing, and mutual support.

Flexibility and resilience are signs of a healthy dynamic in the garden and elsewhere. Life is always in flux, and people's priorities change, but lack of communication about changing needs and intentions can lead to neglected plots and unnecessary delays for people on the garden waiting list.

Music for dancing at a
retirement party in the
Peralta Garden Commons

During our first five years filmmaker Rick Bacigalupi documented our process, including gardeners' struggles as they worked to resolve conflicts and create a comfortable shared space. His wonderful hour-long video "A Lot in Common" is enriched by commentary—that of urban expert and social activist Jane Jacobs, environmentalist Paul Hawken, architect Carl Anthony, British scholar David Crouch, PBS correspondent Ray Suarez, and me. The documentary has aired nationwide on PBS and Free Speech TV and is available from Bullfrog Films.

After many years of elementary school teaching, plot holder
Carole Bennett-Simmons celebrated her retirement with a big party in the garden.

Community members gathered in the garden to begin brainstorming and envisioning the space.

Peralta Community Garden Commons Design

Eager for the most sophisticated ecological and horticultural knowledge, I invited Penny Livingston, founder/director of the Northern California Permaculture Institute, and horticulturist Reynaldo Cortez, who helped to develop the Kona Kai market farm in Berkeley, to share their observations on the development of community gardens at the site.

Our most pressing concern was the compacted soil, and they both suggested seeding it with deep-rooting cover crops.

Reynaldo and I both submitted plans at the next neighborhood meeting. Reynaldo suggested a rectilinear layout of planting beds oriented for optimal sun exposure to ensure high crop yield. My submission featured a circular commons inspired by "The Garden of Eden" in Manhattan's Lower

East Side. That garden was later destroyed to make way for construction, and having participated in a failed campaign to save it, I had a strong desire to resurrect it on the West Coast. I envisioned a circular commons area, twenty-one feet in diameter, embraced by two circular raised planting beds of different heights to create an amphitheater-like hearth with S-shaped planting beds that would extend throughout the entire garden.

At the meeting, neighbors expressed eagerness to explore the development of the circular design. And Ray Winnie lifted our spirits playing guitar.

Linda Maio, our city council representative, facilitated our next meeting. Landscape architecture professor Linda Jewell and her gifted former student Meg Calkins, also a neighborhood resident, suggested we organize the plots surrounding the circular beds in a rectilinear grid pattern to be more in harmony with the surrounding urban fabric. Meg's design pleased everyone.

After a few adjustments, we received the necessary approval from BART and the City of Berkeley.

The Garden of Eden in Manhattan

Layout of the circular Peralta Commons

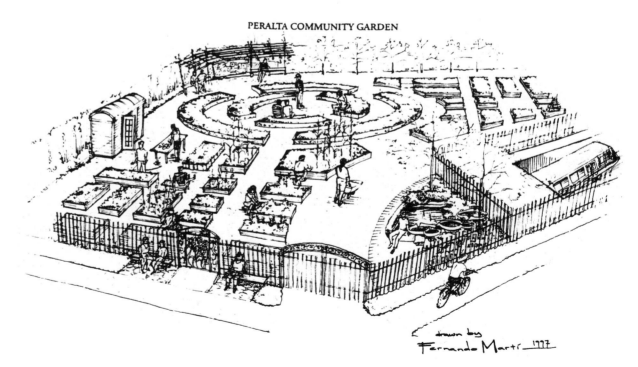

PERALTA COMMUNITY GARDEN

drawn by
Fernando Martí 1997

Receiving free compost from the City of Berkeley

We rented a plow with long chisel blades to loosen the compacted soil and incorporate the compost.

Preparing Soil and Creating Pathways

A neighbor who did not want the lots to become community gardens raised many objections and even threatened us with legal action. We intended to spread compost and plant a deep-rooted cover crop, but the threat of legal action forced us to abandon our plan. Fortunately, during the many months of challenges and opposition, our sense of unity grew stronger. By the time the threat of legal action had faded, the gardeners were eager to prepare their plots and plant their summer gardens. We decided to forego the idea of starting with a cover crop.

Gravel and decomposed granite were delivered and laid out to create networks of wheelchair-accessible pathways.

Karl Linn and Josh, a gardener's grandson, operate a Bobcat, spreading gravel and DG for the pathways.

In late spring we arranged through the Berkeley Community Gardening Collaborative to receive five huge truckloads of compost from the municipal recycling operation—a total of 200 cubic yards. Under the direction of Beebo Turman, the collaborative, which I helped found in 1995, serves as a forum for exchanging skills and information and as a channel for the city and others to provide resources, such as tools and recycled or reusable materials, for school and community gardens.

David Hawkins, garden coordinator for the Edible Schoolyard project at nearby Martin Luther King Junior Middle School, suggested that we engage Ted Dunlap (The Gentleman Farmer) from Sebastopol, who had a special plow with long blades that he had used successfully to loosen their similarly compacted soil and mix in compost. After inspecting our site, Ted brought his plow with its eighteen-inch-long blades and a front-end loader, which he used to scatter an existing heap of soil and thirty-five cubic yards of topsoil donated by landscape contractor Scott Parker. Then Ted distributed the huge black compost piles evenly across the area and raked the compost under with the chisel plow. After the chisel plow operation, he rototilled the area twice, leaving an appealing plowed patch of land.

The next step was to spread gravel and then decomposed granite (DG) on our network of pathways to make them wheelchair-accessible.

After staking their plots, gardeners prepare their planting beds.

Volunteer Neil Collier, owner of Live Oak Landscape, trained the AmeriCorps team members so they could install the irrigation system.

AmeriCorps Volunteers

To manage the construction of the community gardens, we established an implementation team composed of Jim Cisney, Neil Collier, and me. Our plan called for us to build a network of compacted pathways and raised planting beds and to install an irrigation system. Such heavy construction would overtax the gardeners, most of whom hold full-time jobs.

We were fortunate to have two AmeriCorps teams of four or five people each, who worked for five weeks to construct the garden. I was impressed by the high level of awareness of ecological and social justice issues that the Corps members shared in their conversations with one another. Since learning through service is the AmeriCorps mission,

I arranged for volunteer professionals to come to the garden and share their knowledge and expertise with the AmeriCorps volunteers.

We saved money by hooking up with the waterlines in the Karl Linn Community Garden across the street. The City of Berkeley arranged for a Public Works crew to dig a trench to lay the pipes across Peralta Avenue. Neil Collier had two of his crew members operate the machine we rented to dig the trenches in the garden, while some of the strong-bodied AmeriCorps volunteers broke up concrete slabs that were in the way. Installing the waterlines under the sidewalks in both gardens was a tremendous challenge. They used water jets to penetrate the compacted soil and then pushed the pipe with its jet nozzle back and forth, rejoicing tri-

The AmeriCorps team constructs raised redwood planting beds for people in wheelchairs or with back injuries.

umphantly when water finally became visible on the other edge of the sidewalk.

The teams also helped us lay out the garden design on the site from a blueprint, measuring and staking out the pattern of the layout with white ribbon. They set up carpentry equipment on the sidewalk to construct frames for the raised redwood planting beds. These higher, wheelchair-accessible frames were very heavy, and it took a whole team to move them from the sidewalk to the garden. The crew supervisors served as true role models and, not only instructed the group team members, but also involved themselves in all levels of physical activity, no matter how demanding.

The new gardeners, eager to lay claim to their plots, were willing to work hard to finish the construction. However in their eagerness to start planting, some didn't line up the frames of their beds properly. Much to their dismay, they had to change them so that wheelchairs could get by easily.

HopPer Commons Association

As the cluster of community gardens expanded, the association coordinated public use of the commons and assumed responsibility for the upkeep of the artwork and eco-friendly technolo-

gies. HopPer Commons members sponsored workshops and solicited memberships from neighbors and others interested in using and supporting the commons. Herb Weber led the group—organizing open hours, setting ground rules for public use, and overseeing events held in the commons. By 2005, the scope of the projects had broadened, and Friends of the Westbrae Commons replaced the HopPer Commons Association.

All the art in the gardens was donated, but, in some cases, funding for materials came from Berkeley's Civic Arts Commission, BART, and private foundations. Berkeley Partners for Parks, a citywide nonprofit devoted to supporting parks and open space, served as our fiscal agent for grants and tax-deductible donations from the beginning.

Christine Tesch inspects her planting bed.

Pond and Solar-Powered Flowform Fountain

We dug a pond at the entrance to the Peralta Garden, overlooking the BART trains as they traveled in and out of the tunnel. With excavated soil, we formed a berm around the amoeba-shaped pond. Local businesses either donated or heavily discounted materials. We installed three Flowform fountain basins, made especially for us by Jennifer Greene and Chris Hecht of Waterforms, Inc. and the Water Research Institute of Blue Hill.

Observing Flowforms in action can give one a deep feeling of peace and equilibrium, and children enjoy the rhythmically enhanced water flow. As efficient oxygenators, larger Flowforms have also functioned effectively in effluent treatment facilities and in the rehabilitation of ponds. Preliminary observations show that Flowform-treated water generates healthier and larger plants. A sign attached to the fence next to the pond explains the history and science of Flowforms.

Solar-powered Flowform
fountain

Lush landscaping, a Flowform
fountain, and "Flower"
by French sculptor
Loren Fenaille grace
the edges of the new pond.

BEEBO TURMAN

Tibetan Prayer Flags, aka "Happy Flags"

One day, shortly before a meeting of the gardeners, Milo Clark showed up with long bamboo poles and set up a workshop on the main walkway, where he tied the poles together with thin nylon yarn. He expressed his desire to erect a fifty-two-foot bamboo pole with a string of Tibetan prayer flags attached to it. He saw the garden as a peaceful place, receptive to the prayers and good wishes the flags would cast in the wind. The gardeners were delighted with Milo's suggestion and called the prayer flags "happy flags" to avoid affiliating themselves with a particular religion.

Happy Flags imbue the garden with a very special ambiance of celebration, tangibly and symbolically expressing the spirit of all who participated in building it.

Raising Happy Flags required coordinated effort.

© EDWARD CALDWELL

The pond four years after construction.

Toolshed Construction

Architect George Elvin and his wife, landscape architect Meg Calkins, came up with an ingenious idea for a toolshed. To meet BART's requirement that any structure on the lot be temporary or moveable, they would place the shed on ten-inch concrete pedestals.

George designed the shed to be built with recycled or sustainably harvested lumber. We solicited donations of materials from local suppliers, and George incorporated scraps and mill trimmings into a unique design. For the studs and rafters he used salvaged two-by-fours.

Construction proceeded much like a traditional barnraising, bringing together the large group needed to erect it. When our neighbor complained that it was right in front of her window, fifteen people assembled to lift and move the heavy toolshed away from her view.

Garden members and volunteers build the frame for the toolshed from salvaged and sustainably harvested timber.

Meg Calkins and George Elvin install the roof of the toolshed.

The shed houses garden tools, art equipment, and gardening books.

The Snake Bench

As a result of visiting Antoni Gaudí's Park de Quell in Spain in 1962, I was eager to include a mosaic-covered bench in the commons. I will always remember the moment, leaving Gaudí's park, when my five-year-old son turned and exclaimed, "good-bye, fairyland!" I showed colored photos of Gaudí's benches in that park to Dmitry Grudsky, a recent immigrant from the former Soviet Union, who had made huge sculptures in public plazas. I was pleased when he offered to create for us an undulating mosaic-covered "snake" bench. He has always been inspired, he says, "by nature's beautiful patterns and structures, and especially by the graceful movement of its creatures." The bench surrounding the circular commons is one of the garden's most significant works of art.

Constructing the bench was laborious. AmeriCorps volunteers and others built a rebar structure covered with wire mesh, upon which they troweled a layer of concrete. Friends volunteered to break tiles, donated by several manufacturers, into small mosaic pieces, which Dmitry glued to the surface of the bench and filled with grout. Funding for building materials came from the Mini-Projects Fund of Berkeley's Department of Parks and Waterfront.

The bench is composed of three segments, which line up with the inner beds and the three entrances to the commons. The heavy segments could never be hand lifted. Initially we intended to subdivide each segment into movable sections,

Dmitry Grudsky works with AmeriCorps volunteers to construct rebar structures for the three-part "Snake Bench" that defines the circular commons in the Peralta Garden.

because, according to our contract with BART, we were not allowed to install permanent structures in the garden. But bending and tying the rebar was so difficult that additional segmentation would have overtaxed our available human energy. We took our chances, reasoning that sometimes it's better to ask forgiveness than permission. We were happy when Desha Hill, director of BART's Real Estate Department, admired the vibrancy and high aesthetic quality of the mosaic bench and asked if she could bring her staff to the garden for a picnic, which she did. The question of the removability of the bench never became an issue.

We showed the garden to Patrick Kennedy, a developer who has constructed many significant buildings in Berkeley. He was so intrigued with Dmitry's mosaic-covered undulating "Snake Bench," Amy Blackstone's "Sunflower Gate," and Fran Segal's multicolored slate mural "In the Eyes of a Red-Tailed Hawk" (in the background on the facing page), that he commissioned them to add their work to the mixed-use ArtTech Building he was erecting in downtown Berkeley. This reinforced my belief that community art gardens can serve as outdoor galleries.

BEEBO TURMAN

The bench forms the central commons in the garden and has the look and feel of an undulating snake.

Behind the Peralta Garden Commons is a slate mural and a bamboo arbor.

Fran Segal cuts each piece on site.

"In the Eyes of the Red-tailed Hawk"

Artist Fran Segal, who participated in the early planning meetings with the gardeners, designed a multicolored slate mural, "In the Eyes of the Red-tailed Hawk."

Besides being an artist, Fran is an ecopsychologist who takes people on wilderness trips. Her work with slate focuses on creating art that enhances our experience of belonging to a world larger than ourselves. She uses imagery that captures the spirit of nature indigenous to the place where the work is installed. Her goal is to create a common bond with the creatures in the local environment and a sense of place-based community when the space is shared.

It took quite a while before we received a grant from Berkeley's Art Commission to purchase the materials for Fran, who worked without pay. With meticulous care, she set up a workshop in the garden, cutting each piece of slate to fit into the mosaic composition.

Fran attaches each piece to the wall.

The completed mural.

Constructing the Bamboo Arbor

Architect Darrel DeBoer conducted a bamboo construction workshop that we advertised through Architects / Designers / Planners for Social Responsibility (ADPSR), who focus, among other things, on educating people about healthy building materials and systems. Darrel, who is utterly devoted to the use of sustainable building material, guided volunteers over a few weekends in constructing an imaginatively designed bamboo arbor. As in a traditional barnraising, workshop participants joined forces to hoist the arbor into place. They planted California grapes, with leaves that turn a deep red in the fall, to cover the arbor and provide shelter from the summer sun.

Barnraising the arbor—laying bamboo crossbeams

Cloth fastened to the top of the arbor provided shade until vines grew to cover it. Our cheap umbrellas (in the background) were later re-covered with custom-tailored hemp fabric at no cost by Two Star Dog, a local business whose owners were inspired by the garden.

The grapevine-covered arbor provides shade for gardeners taking a break from their work.

© EDWARD CALDWELL

DIANA YOUNG

Ongoing Art Installations in the Gardens

In keeping with the feelings expressed by neighbors during the first planning meeting that works of art should intermingle with the lush vegetation, we invited local artists to exhibit their work in the community garden. Our intent was to install the art pieces in the most fitting settings in the garden, interspersing them with demonstrations of eco-friendly technology.

Artist Alan Leon directed a collaborative mural project, starting by conducting workshops encouraging people to connect with their own creativity, as well as their sense of nature and spirituality. Participants created a series of thumbnail sketches and shared discussion, brainstorming, and envisioning. Alan generously donated his time, receiving a grant from Berkeley's Civic Arts Commission for materials only. The mural was painted using thin layers of pigment and building up the chroma gradually so it would shine from within.

The undulating "Dragon", originally created by Slobodan Dan Paitch and Merritt College students for a Healthy Cities Conference in 1993, is displayed on the fence at the Peralta Garden.

"The Garden as Gateway" represents a vision of the future with the garden leading the way. Installed on the front side of the garden, the mural is visible from the street and emits a strong presence.

Alan Leon engages artists, gardeners, and neighbors in the design and painting of an 8-by-12-foot mural.

Near the toolshed, sculptor Etsuko Sakimura and her husband, Keishu, installed a carved and decorated wooden bench, which she intends to be "a special place that invites the gardener to pause and repose among the fruits of the garden's labor."

The bench offers a view of "Emoclew" and "Shrine Box" (below), two works by Briana Kaufman and Peter Neufeld, well known for their creative use of salvaged materials.

Hang Nguyen's paintings of the four seasons originally graced the four sides of our high-temperature composter, reinforcing the cyclical nature of the composting process. When the composter was removed, the paintings found a new home on the front of the toolshed.

Three artists from the United Clayworkers Guild install their collaborative "Totems" in a raised bed.

"Trouble in Paradise," a digital voice painting, by wheelchair-bound garden plot holder Philip Chavez

Architect David Dobereiner's "Kinetic Spiral Sculpture" spins and swings in the breeze. Paintings were displayed temporarily on the BART fence.

Anthony Ricci loaned "Manitou," a large dynamic sculpture, to the garden, leaving it there for nearly a year.

Temporary Art Installations for the Commons Dedication and Thereafter

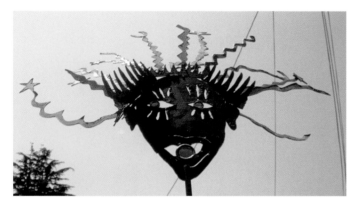

"Goddess" by Amy Blackstone

To enrich the experience of the dedication celebration, we invited artists to create or make available temporary art installations for the occasion.

We typeset and laminated artists' statements next to their artworks. We found that exposure to the artists' thoughts and feelings deepened the viewers' enjoyment and understanding of the work.

Art installations became an ongoing event as more and more local artists realized what an exquisite setting the garden provides for display of their work. Initially, all the gardeners met jointly with the artists, which familiarized the gardeners with the evolution of the art pieces. When the number of gardeners grew, we established an Art Selection Committee that presented the artists' projects to the larger group for final decisions. In a few instances when the gardeners were apprehensive about an art piece, we invited the artists to explain their work to the larger group. The personal presentation often helped the gardeners to understand and accept the artwork.

In May 1999, we staged a Showcase of Art and Eco-friendly Technology to support the artists and inventors who had created permanent installations in the gardens. We also invited artists who had installed temporary works of art for the dedication and new artists whose work had come to our attention. We timed the event to coincide with Bay Area–wide Open Garden Day. It was also listed as part of Berkeley's Festival of the Arts and the American Society of Landscape Architects (ASLA) Centennial Celebration. Coupling the showcase with these public events contributed to the extraordinarily large attendance.

"Us," a rebar sculpture by Josho

Jo Hanson, founder of San Francisco's Recycling Artist-in-Residence program and local grande dame of creative recycling, installed her "Urban Garden," made of decorated bicycle rims transformed into flowers atop ornate, leafy stems. She expressed the hope that "the blooming of my urban flowers will inspire a feeling of valuing materials, conserving them and re-using them—with a feeling of love for the Earth, which is our only source."

"Birds' Own Depot," a tower of nest materials for birds, by Susan Leibovitz Steinman & Andrée Singer Thompson

Andrée Singer Thompson's exquisitely carved wooden ravens in the Peralta Commons. "Raven," she says, "is in this garden as a protective watchful spirit warding off bad luck and as a warning reminder to take care of this earth and its fruitful gifts."

The Garden as an Arena for Deepening Compassion

Joan Sowers, one of the first Peralta Garden plot holders swung a pickaxe like a pro to excavate the pond and drew on her solid knowledge of geometry to help lay out the circular commons and surrounding planting beds. She was a single mother, who often brought her daughter, Amy, to help plant and water. Joan's friendly personality and helpful attitude made her popular with fellow gardeners.

Everyone was shocked when Joan was diagnosed with breast cancer. Yet, amidst her struggle for health, she experienced a tremendous surge of creativity. It seemed that everything she touched became a work of art, including the spider-web weaving to support her climbing beans and intricate, imaginative carvings on gourds, which she decorated with feathers and beads and presented as gifts. At a healing circle she staged in the garden, among beds that overflowed with colorful vegetation and candles that illuminated our faces, Joan observed that just as she had given much energy to the building of the garden, the garden was now giving solace to her.

Sculptor Kitti Shahoian offered to create a sculpture of Joan and Amy. Initially uncomfortable about seeing the sculpture in the garden, Joan eventually had it installed near the pond, as the presence of flowing water was very important to her.

Kitti also volunteered to craft a bronze relief of my face, which was installed on the BART fence.

BEAR KAUFMAN

"Little Girl in My Heart," a bust of Joan and her daughter, was installed in the garden near the pond, which Joan had worked so hard to create.

BEAR KAUFMAN

In a poignant reversal of fate Joan outlived Karl and spoke movingly at a small memorial ceremony shortly after his death about the caring he extended to her after her cancer diagnosis.

Joan decorated gourds she grew in her plot.

Carole Bennett-Simmons (left) and other gardeners at a seed party and planting of native California plants

Native California Plant Collection

A few of the gardeners wanted native California plants in the garden and formed a committee. To provide shade and more privacy for the neighbors, they recommended planting taller natives on the south side of the outer circle of planting beds. To maintain the view and a feeling of openness on the north side of the commons, the plantings were to gradually decrease in size. The outer circle would be devoted to perennial herbs and medicinal plants easily accessible by gardeners, while the inner circle would be planted to invite butterflies and hum-mingbirds. The gardeners also aimed to demon-strate that native plants could provide beauty in the garden while they conserved precious water and required minimal care.

Under the leadership of Carole Bennett-Simmons and Michael Menning, the gardeners formed California Habitat Indigenous Activists (CHIA) to study and share knowledge about propa-gation and cultivation techniques for native plants, the relationships between local plants and wildlife, and ancient and contemporary uses of native plants. Early in its existence the group was blessed with the mentorship of linguist David Drummond, who shared his phenomenal knowledge of native California plants, including many techniques for their preparation and uses as medicine and food.

CHIA served the community by conducting native plant workshops and by providing seeds, cuttings, bulbs, and materials for use in basket making. Because they view indigenous plants as a primary link to the abundant landscape of ancient times, the group has undertaken the restoration of a section of the nearby Ohlone Greenway as coastal prairie habitat. Through the work of restoring their environment, CHIA members feel that they also restore themselves and regain the birthright to be one with nature.

Much to our delight, Mary Schindler, a UC Berkeley graduate student from the Division of Insect Biology, appeared at the garden with Gordon W. Frankie, director of the Bees in Berkeley Program. They were conducting a study of native bees in Berkeley and found that the Peralta Garden was one of a very few sites in Berkeley with an abundance of native bees. They also noted a greater diversity of native bees visiting flowers. "The Peralta Garden had about twenty native bee species visiting a wide variety of exotic and native plant species in any given month, an unusually high diversity for such small sites [Frankie, Gordon; Mary Schindler; et al., "Bees in Berkeley?" 2002, p. 5]."

For me the design process had a lot to do with creating habitat for the creatures that have evolved with the native plants. It took a while for the butterflies, bees, and birds to locate their native ecological plant species, but we see more flutterings each season. —Carole Bennett-Simmons

Michael Menning enjoys getting to know each native plant intimately and learning which plant works best where. His daughter Kayla Rain, who has grown up in the garden, tends to their plot.

Northside Community Garden

Peralta Avenue is a broad, heavily-trafficked street, which makes the Peralta Garden highly visible to the public at large. The adjacent Northside Community Garden is much smaller (one-fourth the size of the Peralta Garden) and, being bordered by quiet, narrow Northside Street, it seemed likely to develop as a more intimate community garden.

Jim Cisney, a landscape architect who lives nearby, agreed to serve as garden coordinator. Northside Garden has fewer art installations, but many of the plots are works of art with beds ingeniously bordered with broken concrete, stones, and cinder blocks. One is framed with curved driftwood, railroad bars, and marine rope.

The Northside Garden gate murals were painted by a Project Yes youth team led by artist Sofie Siegman.

This Northside plot is typical of the innovative and aesthetically pleasing methods gardeners used to frame their beds.

Youth Participatory Art Projects

When I heard that the East Bay Conservation Corps was conducting a Summer Arts Program and was looking for a project, I seized on the opportunity and called Project Yes Coordinator Steve Egawa. He arranged for a team of ten Project Yes youth to work for two weeks with artist Sofie Siegmann. They envisioned and painted murals on both sides of the gate to the Northside Garden; one faced the garden and one faced the neighborhood.

Their cheerful "Insects and Other Beasts" depicts stylized images of the small creatures that live in a garden. When the students finished paint-

Sofie Siegmann worked with a team of Project YES students, who painted a double-sided mural at the entrance to the Northside Garden. She had worked earlier with another group of youth who made a sundial.

ing the murals on plywood, Steve attached the panels to the gates.

Earlier in the summer Sofie worked with another team of young participants from Oakland's inner-city neighborhoods, to create a sundial.

Inspired by the idea that some flowers bloom only at certain times of the day, Sofie created the outlines of petals for the twelve hours. She put the twelve numbers on pieces of paper in a hat and had each student draw one, asking them to picture the most important thing they recalled doing at that hour of the day. Their recollections inspired their designs. After they sketched in the outline Sofie had drawn on the platform, she showed them how to create their images with mosaics.

A sign next to the sundial details each student's inspirations, for example:

6 AM: I made a head of a bird. Sometimes when I wake up at that hour the birds will be singing a song.

1 PM: This is my preferred time to play baseball. I made a diamond-shaped baseball field.

4 PM: A dolphin jumping out of the water, because that's the time I would take my swimming lessons.

Another sign gives a brief history of sundials and instructions on how to read the time.

This community garden has been offered by Karl Linn and the garden community as an opportunity to let nature's joy, beauty, serenity, and love sprout once again in our heavy hearts.... We need to let beauty, joy, and love guide us through the darkness that has befallen our brothers and sisters in Palestine and Israel, a darkness that is shrouding this earth. —Nadine Ghammache

Ceremonial Planting of a Peace Pole

Intisar Morrar and Rabbi Harry Manhoff dedicate the space as the Peralta Community Peace Garden after the planting of the Peace Pole

Members of the East Bay Palestinian-Jewish Dialogue Group gather for the ceremony.

When our hearts open together like this, it actually affects our people.... On one side we have people who are doing things hard for us to even believe.... There is a struggle for the hearts of our people going on. This event here is a prayer. It's a powerful force in changing that, in moving in a loving direction. —Alan Levin

DIANA YOUNG

Peace Pole with inscription, "Peace with Justice," in Arabic, German, Hebrew, and English

Construction of "Troth," a Cob Toolshed

Architect John Fordice spent weekends for about three years conducting workshops on cob construction to build his beautifully designed structure. Cob is an Old English word meaning "a rounded lump or mass." It is an ancient method of building, using a moistened mixture of soil, sand, and straw to construct walls. The plastic, clay-like mixture is stacked in layers on top of a solid foundation. The completed walls are allowed to dry by exposure until a durable, cementitious state is achieved. With a good foundation, good roof, and an exterior earthen plaster layer, a cob building can last for centuries.

John obtained soil for the cob mixture from a large earth dumping yard in the Berkeley Marina, where he carefully scrutinized different piles of earth to find just the right composition. Berkeley's Department of Public Works obligingly transported the soil to the Northside Garden. Gardener Lynn Wilder scoured the local salvage yards and located enough recycled lumber to construct the roof.

Participants mixed the soil and straw by stomping on it with bare feet, an activity that connected them with delightful memories of childhood. Although the work attracted volunteers eager to learn this ancient building method, John frequently worked alone with amazing perseverance and dedication.

Placing the lightweight soil mixture on the sculptural arched roof

Toolshed interior illuminated by the skylight. Every piece of wood was carefully crafted to create the form of the arched roof.

ALL PHOTOS THIS PAGE BY DAVID DOBEREINER

The roof is protected by a rubber lining donated and installed by Tom Bressan, the proprietor of the Urban Farmer Stores. The sod and plants that make up the living roof add beauty and also protect the interior from extremes of temperature.

Rear view of cob shed with profuse wildflower blossoms on the roof

The building is named TROTH to tell us in a word that here is a place of beauty, devoted to the earth and to the legacy of creative wealth from past generations in the form of tools we take for granted and time-proven and respectful ways of building with the earth, which we have used to create it. —John Fordice

DAVID DOBEREINER

Two hundred people join hands in a ceremony dedicating "Troth."

The newly constructed solar garden shed, built by a class of UC Berkeley environmental design students and community volunteers over a series of weekends. Located on the Peralta Avenue edge of the EcoHouse lot, its windows give passers-by a peek at the solar batteries and inverter. The small window on the right shows what's inside the wall—bales of straw!

The decorative metal grates over the windows, crafted by Amy Blackstone, protect the solar equipment from theft or vandalism. Four years after construction the grates also served as support for the native California red-flowering currant, *Ribes sanguineum*.

Berkeley EcoHouse

Ecological Demonstration Home and Garden

Berkeley, California, 1999

For years, community gardeners voiced growing alarm about poisonous lead paint flakes peeling off a small, deteriorating residential building adjacent to the Karl Linn Community Garden. Neighbors expressed fears that the unsightly building might become a haven for illicit activities. Envisioning the house as a place where gardeners and neighbors could gather, I shared my hopes with our city council representative Linda Maio whenever she came to visit the garden. One day a real estate developer approached me as I was working in the garden and asked if I knew who owned the building. Alarmed, I contacted Linda and various environmental activists and community members. Out of our dialogue a vision emerged of the house with its oversized lot becoming an environmental demonstration home

and garden. The property, adjacent to the three flourishing community garden commons and the Ohlone Greenway (a major pedestrian and bicycle path), seemed an ideal setting to demonstrate ecological living in an urban area.

Linda suggested that we make an offer on the building right away, which her son did on our behalf, and she fronted the money for a down payment. Fortunately I had met the owner and given him a tour of the community gardens and their commons. Impressed by our efforts, he was favorably disposed to accept the offer.

A group of volunteers developed a prospectus to solicit two-year loans at five percent interest, to purchase the property and restore the house. The Berkeley City Council agreed to guarantee the loans. Contact with friends and a newspaper media campaign led twenty-three people to loan us $240,000. We turned away ten potential lenders because we had reached our goal. In April 1999, we purchased the house for $190,000. The surplus and a $15,000 long-term loan from the City of Berkeley financed the restoration of the building and assured payment of interest to our lenders.

To take possession of the property we had to establish a corporation in the State of California, and we named it Berkeley EcoHouse. Until we became a tax-exempt non-profit corporation, the Northern California Land Trust served as our fiscal agent. Team member Teresa Clark had worked with the Trust for many years, developing affordable housing projects. Realtor (and later Berkeley City Council person) Laurie Capitelli kindly volunteered his services in processing the sale.

The house had suffered from water and termite damage, and someone had stripped the kitchen floor to the studs. A design and construction team formed. Volunteer architects Greg VanMechelen and Mark Gorrell prepared drawings and specifications. Eco-carpenter Babak Tondre scavenged for salvageable building materials. Chris Polk, a contractor known for his craftsmanship, was selected through a competitive bidding process. He shared our environmental and social values.

The restoration came in considerably under budget, in part due to the use of recycled or reclaimed materials such as Douglas fir flooring and a donated energy-efficient refrigerator from a house that was about to be demolished, a donated stove, and kitchen cabinets purchased from Urban Ore, a local salvage depot. Professionals performed a lead abatement process, and the house was attractively repainted, using recycled paint for the exterior and zero-VOC paint inside. Workers insulated the walls with blown-in cellulose from old newspapers, refinished wood floors, and laid natural linoleum on the bathroom floor. They installed a high-efficiency gas heater, high-efficiency lighting, and an on-demand hot water heater. In the backyard they installed a reclaimed fence, creating a fenced-in area for tenants and space for a demonstration permaculture garden. A generous grant from the Petty Foundation covered the purchase and installation of a solar electric system, which supplies all the home's energy and sends excess kilowatts back to the grid on the sunniest days.

Once the house became habitable, we looked for temporary tenants who would show the house periodically and be willing to leave once we succeeded in obtaining permanent funding for the building. Some of the lenders became donors, some donated their interest, and we took a mortgage to repay the remaining loans. Income from the monthly rent covers mortgage payments, taxes, and maintenance.

Program Directions

During brainstorming sessions on program development, people voiced their special interests and concerns. After much dialogue we committed ourselves to seven specific program directions, each guided by a particular board member:

- Eco-justice—provide resources and information to low-income individuals and communities to increase their capacity for more sustainable lifestyles and fuller participation in society.

Babak Tondre introduces students to the permaculture demonstration garden.

Hal Aronson explains the marvel of photovoltaics to students at Martin Luther King Junior Middle School.

The students learn "sheet mulching," a favorite permaculture soil-building technique that involves placing wet newspaper and cardboard on top of compostable materials.

- Ecological Building—demonstrate photovoltaics, solar hot water, solar greenhouse heating and cooling, daylighting, composting toilets, and graywater recycling.
- Sustainable Building Materials—demonstrate environmentally responsible and nontoxic products and processes.
- Organic Gardening and Permaculture—maintain a demonstration garden and organize workshops.
- Community Outreach—offer education about solar energy and cob construction.
- Healthy Living—provide information on nutrition and healthy household products and practices.
- Eco-culture—stage cultural events, workshops, retreats, and forums to foster understanding among people of diverse backgrounds.

Naturally our efforts to improve the quality and appearance of the property accelerate the process of gentrification. To offset this homogenizing and displacing impact as much as possible, we have supported affordable housing programs and worked successfully to include preservation of open space for community gardening in Berkeley's General Plan.

Community Outreach

We envisioned EcoHouse as a living laboratory offering information and consultation on ecological design and construction techniques and products to architects, developers, contractors, landscape architects, and gardeners and exposure to ecological practices for groups of students and other visitors. It will be capable of accommodating educational programs, exhibits, and small workshops and engaging the immediate neighborhood as well as the community at large. Once the monthly rental income is no longer required, one of the demonstration rooms should be available for occasional meetings of small groups of gardeners and neighbors, especially during rainy days. Since neighborhood blocks are fundamental elements in the urban fabric, the development of a successful neighborhood community within the EcoHouse block can serve as an effective prototype to be emulated elsewhere.

Ongoing contact with neighbors about the progress of EcoHouse through leaflets, neighbor-

Students finish the sheet mulching by covering the layers with straw.

63

hood meetings, and personal contact aim to encourage their growing participation in our programs. Frequent interactions between EcoHouse team members and the multicultural and economically diverse gardeners at the Northside, Peralta, and Karl Linn Community Gardens have nurtured a growing sense of neighborhood community, instilling a deepened sense of safety and belonging.

Solar Energy Education in the Schools

In 2001, with funding from the Center for Ecoliteracy, Hal Aronson started our first outreach program, engaging local middle- and high-school students in hands-on projects using the sun for energy, water heating, and cooking. They sharpen their math skills calculating seasonal sun angles, design and build models of solar-heated homes, and use photovoltaic solar panels to power music systems, toys, lights, and irrigation pumps. Hal created solar technology kits and curriculum for teachers and a traveling photovoltaic power station that goes from school to school.

EcoHouse also sponsored California Youth Energy Services (CYES), a project that trains high school students to perform energy audits in the homes of the disabled and seniors and at homeless shelters. They then retrofit those homes for energy and water conservation, installing compact fluorescent light bulbs, weatherstripping, and pipe insulation. The students improved energy conservation at hundreds of homes, resulting in huge energy and dollar savings.

Permaculture and Organic Gardening

On the land surrounding the house, Babak Tondre, one of our original board members, developed a demonstration garden and nursery featuring permaculture and other organic gardening methods. It showcases effective gardening practices for neighbors, community gardeners, and the general public. Permaculture is an approach to landscape design and livelihoods based on indigenous wisdom, modern technology, and observation of natural ecosystems. It follows natural patterns and aims to create the greatest possible yield with the least amount of labor.

The garden incorporates composting and soil building strategies, a greenhouse nursery, an orchard of fruit and nut trees (many of which are espaliered), cultivation of mushrooms and heirloom food crops, seed saving, water catchment, natural building projects, and electricity from solar panels. Two ducks in the garden not only help control snails, slugs, and weeds while enriching the soil, but also attract children. The front yard features drought-tolerant landscaping with native California plants. EcoHouse hosts work parties, tours, and monthly or bimonthly workshops on permaculture, organic gardening, graywater, and more.

Green Building

UC Berkeley environmental design students constructed a solar garden shed in the spring of 2000 in a course taught by architect David Arkin and landscape architect Randy Hester—"Building the Small Urban Ecology." The 85-square-foot shed on Peralta Avenue between EcoHouse and the Karl Linn Garden incorporates salvaged materials (wood, windows, and door), walls demonstrating a variety

This wall was constructed of recycled wood, reinforced with bamboo sticks, insulated with a mixture of clay, straw, and water, then coated with a mixture of clay, cement, and water, and finally given a varnish to protect the surface from wind and rain.

A vision of additional ecological building and home management features to be developed at EcoHouse

of environmentally friendly techniques, an "urbanite" (concrete sidewalk masonry) foundation, and a living roof of drought-resistant succulents. They framed the structure with salvaged wood posts and used a variety of natural building techniques for the four walls.

The shed houses the EcoHouse solar-electric batteries and inverter, seeds, and garden tools. There is space for a composting toilet, a much-needed amenity that will allow the community gardeners to work without disruption. The class also installed a small pond as part of a city-approved graywater system with constructed wetlands.

Another EcoHouse-sponsored program was the Cob Convergence. After completing the cob toolshed in the Northside Garden, John Fordice engaged teachers, parents, and students in building a cob greenhouse at Malcolm X Elementary School.

Future Vision

In the fall of 2005, after lengthy consideration, EcoHouse became a project of the Ecology Center, which has operated since 1969 as a resource center and incubator for environmental projects. EcoHouse benefits from the organizational strength, administrative resources, and vast public outreach of the Ecology Center, who gain access to a physical center where real demonstrations and hands-on learning can take place. Key EcoHouse board members joined with representatives of the Ecology Center board and staff to form an EcoHouse Committee to plan additions to the property and continue developing EcoHouse as a model community resource center.

EcoHouse team members continue to collaborate with grassroots organizations, public agencies, private organizations, businesses, and individuals and to develop programs. At the heart of the EcoHouse mission is the work of bringing together students and others to explore ecological practices and livelihoods so that they may take what they have learned into other households and neighborhoods. At the same time EcoHouse can serve as a commons for neighbors and community gardeners.

The students installed a salvaged window to create a trombe wall, which absorbs solar heat and releases it into the shed. Later the window was replaced with a small greenhouse.

65

The mural "From Elk Tracks to BART Tracks" depicts the history of the neighborhood from pre-settlement to the present and inspires passers-by to stop, reflect, and converse.

Ohlone Greenway Commons

Barnraising an Interpretive Exhibit of the Natural and Cultural History of the Westbrae Neighborhood

Berkeley, California, 1999

After nearly a decade of collaborative work on the community garden commons, our working team of volunteer professionals, neighbors, and community gardeners began envisioning a new project—to create an interpretive exhibit illustrating the natural and cultural history of the neighborhood, thus animating a section of the Ohlone Greenway adjacent to the gardens. Once a spur of the transcontinental railway system and later part of the Key System streetcar line, this publicly owned greenway is a popular trail used daily by walkers, joggers, recreational and commuting bicyclists, people in wheelchairs, skateboarders, and roller skaters.

I had long been inspired by architect Dolores Hayden's work in urban Los Angeles using public art to tell the stories of the place and its inhabitants. We were also motivated by a desire to participate in the American Society of Landscape Architects' (ASLA) "100 Parks Program," celebrating ASLA's Centennial by creating opportunities for local landscape architects to donate design services to community projects. The Northern California ASLA chapter was eager to enter the three community gardens, but they were ineligible because their design had been completed. To qualify, we decided to add the development of an interpretive exhibit on the greenway. Over a dozen interested professionals and friends came together for brainstorming sessions every other week, sifting through ideas and forming subcommittees. Other individuals researched

John Dennis supervises one of the young artists placing tiles on the mortar. A recess was prepared to allow the tiles to lie flush with the bench surface.

Ted Vorster and John Dennis stack and secure cinderblocks for the Peralta Gateway.

Interpretive panels, made of ZED, a strong, water-resistant, embedded-digital material, were mounted on the structure with information about the Peralta family.

and sketched project ideas. Gradually a core group emerged, along with a theme of transportation and migration. Participants listened to one another attentively and with respect, and we arrived at consensus decisions and resolved differences amiably. Though often exhausted by the lengthy meetings, we parted with an encouraging sense of accomplishment, good feelings, and smiles. When we learned that BART owns the western section of the Ohlone Greenway and the City of Berkeley owns the eastern section, we approached city agencies and BART departments for permits and funding.

We used a grant from the Berkeley Civic Arts Commission for community outreach—to produce brochures, flyers, outdoor display panels, and educational exhibits. Team member John Dennis worked closely with Berkeley's Historical Society and conducted oral history interviews with neighbors and former residents. This elicited experiences of the people who have historically used the space. John soon became a respected neighborhood historian and authored a booklet on the natural and cultural history of the Westbrae neighborhood.

The volunteer professionals on our team applied themselves rigorously to program development, design, and construction and built a track record of growing trust with local residents, Berkeley city agencies, and BART.

Our collaboration and friendly personal interactions with representatives of BART, the City of Berkeley, and the Open Circle Foundation went beyond their generous fiscal sponsorship and made the installation of these public art projects a truly rewarding experience.

Peralta Gateway and Interpretive Exhibit

Because the three community art gardens and Berkeley EcoHouse all converge at the foot of Peralta Avenue, near the southern entrance to the Westbrae section of the Ohlone Greenway, it seemed appropriate to build our first public art installation there and to commemorate the Peralta family, who held the land grant for this area during the Californiano-Hispanic period. We had qualms about memorializing those who dispossessed and exploited the Ohlone and other indigenous popula-

Under the direction of Jennifer Burke, children at the Youth Artists' Workspace made colorful, hand-painted tiles depicting motifs inspired by the history of this period. The tiles were embedded in the surface of a bench attached to the structure.

PEG SKORPINSKI

The Peralta Gateway marks the beginning of the Ohlone Greenway Natural and Cultural History exhibit.

tions, many of whom had inhabited the area for at least 10,000 years, but we felt that the Peralta story was an important link in the chain of events from pre-colonization to the present. And we were not yet prepared to develop the Ohlone exhibit, which we knew would be the most important and challenging component.

Jack Appleyard, an architect whose firm specializes in signage, assumed leadership for the project. He and volunteer engineer Suresh Acharya prepared the construction drawings. John Dennis and another team member, landscape architect Ted Vorster, built the structure with concrete blocks and covered it with an adobe-like mixture of quarry fines, cement, and water, which was fun to apply since it had to be thrown in

lumps at the structure.

The Peralta Gateway is a columnar adobe-like structure with a curved red-tile roof. A grant from Berkeley's Parks & Recreation Commission Mini-Projects Fund provided the money to build the structure, but not enough to add the interpretive signage panels. Fortuitously we received an inquiry from BART about scheduling a visit to the garden by delegates to a nationwide conference on transportation systems, hosted by BART. We took advantage of the opportunity to request funding to complete the Peralta Gateway in time for the visit. BART provided funding for a major part of the next two exhibits we had envisioned and seed money for the exhibit commemorating the Ohlone peoples.

Agricultural Era Exhibit

About a year later, farther down the Greenway at the Northside Street cul-de-sac, we built the Agricultural Era Exhibit, commemorating the first farm in Berkeley, established nearby in 1852 by Irishman Michael Curtis. The existing cluster of ornamental pear trees seemed an ideal environment for four steel silhouettes of cows who graze in the background of the exhibit and for the installation of swiveling facsimiles of old metal tractor seats on which visitors can stop and rest in the shade.

The cows were the brainchild of Ted Vorster, who had heard stories from old-time residents about cows escaping their pens and soiling the newly laid sidewalks and gardens of the emerging residential neighborhood. Sculptor Amy Blackstone crafted the cows, working closely with engineer and garden plot holder Suresh Acharya. Sculptor David Friedheim created the swiveling tractor seats with their whimsical bug-like curved legs. Berkeley's Parks & Recreation Commission Mini-Projects Fund, BART, and the Open Circle Foundation funded the project jointly.

Douglas Walters, gardener, handyman, and frequent helper, steadies "Ferdinand" as he is moved from the delivery truck that transported the cows from Amy Blackstone's workshop in San Francisco to their "pasture" on the Ohlone Greenway. We enjoyed naming the four cows, each of whom has a distinctive personality.

The white-painted wooden rail we attached to a row of existing metal bollards evokes the farm fences of the agricultural period and also protects the exhibit from cars.

Nearby homeowners expressed concern that providing seating would encourage loitering, but these facsimiles of old tractor seats allayed their apprehensions. The whimsically designed seats with curved insect-like legs provide a compact sociability setting that makes it possible for the area to function as a commons.

Neighbors and passers-by enjoy the shaded sitting area.

To help with heavy labor I solicited Berkeley's Department of Public Works, who sent a backhoe and a few men to excavate a strip in front of the exhibit for the installation of decomposed granite pavement. We used the excavated soil to level a depression along the greenway that during the rainy season became a lagoon. In addition we hired two day laborers who assisted in the heavy work of excavation and grading for the decomposed granite pavement and helped loosen compacted soil and incorporate soil amendments for planting beds. To minimize weeds and preserve moisture, we covered the planting area with a heavy layer of wood chips.

Neighbors provided access to water and electricity and agreed to water the plantings. Getting involved helped consolidate their sense of neighborhood block community. When we saw that neighbors had hung bells around the cows' necks, heard people mooing at the cows, and watched children playing "milk the cow," we realized that the exhibit had animated the greenway and contributed to it becoming a commons.

"From Elk Tracks to BART Tracks"

Our next project was the creation of a six by seventy-two foot mural, which we mounted along the greenway on cement board to the concrete wall that supports the BART rails at the Nielsen Street cul-de-sac, just south of Gilman Street. Since the route of the greenway has long served as a transportation corridor, the theme for the mural became the evolution of transportation along the greenway and the people these systems brought to the Westbrae neigh-

The pre-settlement and Ohlone periods

The Californiano-Ranchero period

The agricultural period

The industrial era

borhood. Titled "From Elk Tracks to BART Tracks" and funded by Art for BART, the mural portrays a timeline that begins with the pre-settlement period, extends through the Native-American, Spanish, Gold Rush, Victorian, street car–suburban, pre- and post–World War II periods, and culminates in the contemporary era with BART. Team members and experts engaged in extensive discussions to ensure accuracy of the historical information communicated in the mural, which was designed and painted by Alan Leon with assistance of local artists. The mural offers a pictoral history of the place and delights children and young people, who find themselves depicted in such activities as skateboarding and bicycling.

A growing number of people began to hang out around the mural, sitting on the retaining wall

The neighborhood today

across from it. Some musicians played South American music and a dancer expressed eagerness to choreograph a performance based on the historical sequence in the mural. Many people walked right up to the mural, so to protect it we dug an arc-shaped planting bed against the wall, which keeps viewers at arm's length, and installed an appealing, sand-like surface of decomposed granite on which they can stand. As time goes by the native bunchgrasses in the planting bed seem more and more like an integral part of the mural.

California Habitats Indigenous Activists (CHIA)

CHIA began in the Peralta Community Art Garden when a group of community gardeners, educators, historians, and native plant specialists created a demonstration garden of native California plants, including some rare and endangered species. They began saving seeds and propagating new plants. Retired elementary-school teacher Carole Bennett-Simmons has been a driving force in CHIA's native plant restoration efforts. She is inspired by the butterflies, bees, and birds who are attracted to the

73

CHIA volunteers installed bunchgrasses and wildflowers to re-create original prairie habitat on both sides of the walkway.

garden by their traditional plant companions.

Michael Menning's first try at gardening in his Peralta Community Garden plot blossomed into a passion for propagating native plants. He became an avid seed collector, supplying CHIA with the difficult-to-buy seeds of local native plants. His unwavering commitment to the work of restoration and his contagious excitement while learning and teaching others about the unique needs and qualities of each plant have attracted dozens of neighborhood volunteers.

One of CHIA's first projects was the restoration of the landscape along the Ohlone Greenway, starting with the area around the Peralta Gateway. Their goal is to re-create a coastal prairie habitat of bunchgrasses and wildflowers like that which existed in pre-European times. Individuals have taken responsibility for maintaining each section of the planting.

Two Dedication Ceremonies

When we learned, in the summer of 2002, that the mural would be the last project that Art for BART could fund, due to budget cuts, we staged two celebratory events to express our appreciation for their generous fiscal support and the gracious cooperative spirit of their staff. We held the first celebration on a weekday and invited BART officials and board members, Berkeley's mayor, a few city council members, a county commissioner, and representatives of the foundations who had supported construction of the three exhibits. The event allowed us to show

our appreciation and to demonstrate that funding of public art is a great investment in public relations. To the second celebration, held on a Sunday afternoon, we invited neighbors, gardeners, and the many volunteers who had contributed to the creation of the exhibits.

We had concerns that the native California plants surrounding the commons, ablaze with color during spring and summer, looked now as if they were dying. To help the guests appreciate that the plants had entered their seed-bearing phase and were producing a new supply of seeds for our revegetation efforts, we created a display titled "The Aesthetics of Seediness," which included images of the plants in their springtime flowering stage. We also distributed copies of a poem that Carole Bennett-Simmons composed and read:

"The Ebb and Flow of How Plants Grow in California"

Spring's bright blossoms in Summer fade
(Except a few that live in shade).
The people sigh, "It looks so dry!"
The birds reply, "It's time for seeds, that's why!"

The banquet for seed-eaters has just begun
When plants set seed in Summer sun.
California plants take a rest in dry hot Fall.
Winter rains will awaken them one and all.

Winter is the growing season.
Plenty of rain is all the reason.

The Ohlone Installation

Planning for the installation honoring the Ohlone people took several years. We wanted to involve Native American artists, particularly Ohlones, in creating an exhibit that would realistically convey their past and present struggles and their aspirations. As Coyote Hills Regional Park in nearby Fremont is the center of contemporary cultural life for Ohlone descendants in the East Bay, we contacted anthropologist, naturalist, and park ranger Bev Ortiz, who teaches native California crafts there. She welcomed us and introduced us to members of the Ohlone community. After visiting the reconstructed Ohlone village in Coyote Hills, our team members volunteered to help with the restoration of some of the structures. Ohlone village members were eager to consult on the development of our exhibit, and a very cooperative spirit emerged between the groups as they solidified their relationship of mutual support.

Fran Segal, who created the slate mural, "In the Eyes of the Red-tailed Hawk," at the Peralta Garden, submitted a design proposal we all felt had a lot of merit, but we wanted to open the design process to the Ohlone community without generating competitive tensions. At the suggestion of Malcolm Margolin, Ohlone expert and publisher of *News from Native California*, we hired Native American art consultant Janeen Antoine to help us reach out to the Ohlone community and identify artists.

Inspired by the project, Janeen spent additional time as part of the volunteer team. The group met regularly and began to conceptualize elements of the exhibit, such as an oak tree, a grinding stone for acorn preparation, and a bear sculpture. Through this process Fran's design evolved into a sculptural bench.

Janeen introduced us to the well-known Tongva/Ajachmem artist L. Frank Manriquez, whom we invited to our next meeting. She and Janeen had noticed that the red posts of the fence resembled a traditional ceremonial headdress of red flicker feathers. L. Frank suggested creating an oversized sculpture of a hairpin, the ceremonial head ornament worn by tribal dancers in central and northern California, and submitted a sketch at our next meeting. We were intrigued by her idea but unsure about how it could be constructed. Serendipitously

Richard Seals studies the fabricated hairpin "feathers" before installation.

The hairpin sculpture, which vibrates with each passing BART train, powerfully evokes dance as a central element in American Indian culture.

PEG SKORPINSKI

The decoration of this sculptural bench was inspired by Ohlone traditions.

PEG SKORPINSKI

at a friend's birthday party I met Richard Seals, a metal quality control engineer. Inspired by the idea of the hairpin he agreed to serve as a consultant on the project. Gradually it became clear that he was the most qualified to actually interpret the sketch and fabricate the sculpture.

Constructing a feathered hairpin out of metal at many times its usual size stretched the limits of the material and the principles of engineering. Grappling with the challenge and pushing against the boundaries of the known activated his creativity. In collaboration with Suresh Acharya, our volunteer engineer, Richard was able to install the city's donated lamp post upside down to support the sculpture and mimic the structure of a feather. Richard contracted with Matt Reynoso to paint the metal pieces and enlisted the support of master craftsman Daryl Rush, who provided mentoring and access to his extraordinarily well-equipped workshop.

When this train comes by, the hairpin can fill the sky and kind of tremble. And thereby the dancers are always dancing. In case you don't know this, if ever the dancers, the indigenous people of your area, stop dancing, then you're in really big trouble. Because they take care of the Earth. They renew the Earth…. [The hairpin] is really just to show how alive we are…. We are alive and we are dancing. —L. Frank Manriquez

The bench Fran designed was constructed by architect Craig Henritzy, principal of Studio of Indigenous Designs, using pieces of a reclaimed polystyrene product that he salvaged and recycled. Into Craig's sculpted curvilinear bench Fran embedded symbolic mosaic artwork echoing patterns utilized in basket weaving and including symbols of animals

referred to in traditional stories. As the project progressed, Fran and Craig met with members of the Ohlone community, to get feedback and suggestions.

Craig listened to the Ohlone people describe the importance of shells in their traditional culture and developed a decorative motif along the bottom of the bench, adapted from a skirt design and made with shells. He collected the shells from Spenger's Seafood Restaurant, the site of one of three ancient shell mounds that once defined the topography of the East Bay shore line.

Much to our delight many American Indians attended the dedication ceremony held October 10, 2004, including Carol, the widow of beloved activist Bill Wahapepah, and two of their sons. L. Frank opened the celebration with a song and then introduced elder Ann Marie Sayers, who welcomed participants to Costanoan-Ohlone Territory. She spoke of the indigenous peoples' amazing survival, despite genocidal governmental policies, and described current efforts to revitalize tribal languages. "This exhibit recognizes the existence of the Ohlone people," she said, "and I cannot tell you how important it is for the ancestral spirits, whose land we are on right now. That acknowledgment is extremely

L. Frank Manriquez emceed the dedication ceremony, opening and closing the gathering with traditional songs.

L. Frank Manriquez, Karl, and Janeen Antoine

important." Rencho Wahapepah spoke briefly about his father, and I distributed copies of "The Architecture of Peace," a speech Bill gave to architecture students at an event I organized in 1984.

Before the ceremony ended, Herb Weber, HopPer Commons Association coordinator, extended honorary memberships to the Ohlone people in the Peralta Community Peace Garden where the reception was held. Participants enjoyed a light picnic while Walter Johnson, a Potowatomi flutist, performed several musical pieces. The exhibit is located on the greenway at the Neilsen Street cul-de-sac, opposite the first section of the mural, which depicts the millennia of Ohlone habitation. It includes a coast live oak tree, which was probably the most important food source for the native peoples in this region. Underneath the tree is a pounding stone that symbolizes the tradition of acorn preparation. Landscape architect Ted Vorster worked with Carole, Michael, and the CHIA crew to install native vegetation and plants that the Ohlone people used as food, medicine, and building materials. Three exhibit panels provide a brief history of the Ohlone

in images and text that acknowledge their decimation by European immigration, stress the resilience of the people and their culture, and represent their contemporary presence in the Bay Area.

A major goal of the Ohlone Natural and Cultural History Interpretive Exhibit has been to foster the growth of civic identity among diverse neighborhood residents by telling the story of this particular place and its inhabitants in an engaging manner, giving people a deeper appreciation of the place where they live and how others lived here before them. The exhibit also strengthens community by providing opportunities for socializing around the art installations, some of which include outdoor seating. The animation of the greenway with artful historic interpretation has stimulated interaction among people, who use it not only as a thoroughfare but also as a neighborhood commons. A secondary goal of this prototypical project is to inspire people to "animate" the often neglected landscape and inform it with local indigenous influence, human and otherwise, often overlooked but so important to recognize and reclaim.

Costanoan-Ohlone elder Ann Marie Sayers (in red) led the dedication ceremony (artist L. Frank Manriquez behind her on the right). Janeen Antoine held the burning sage. Lori Taguma, Berkeley Civic Arts Commissioner (left of Janeen), and other American Indian leaders and activists participated.

LASTING COMMONS

During the early and middle 1960s, with rising creative energies, citizens and government officials engaged in the shared pursuit of a just society. Lawmakers initiated social reform through the New Frontiers, Great Society, War on Poverty, and Model Cities programs and began to respond to the growing civil rights movement. An upsurge of social and spiritual consciousness among young people inspired the formation of the Peace Corps.

I had become increasingly aware that my work designing landscapes of affluence during the 1950s contributed not only to social stratification but also to the isolation of women and children in the wealthy enclaves of nuclear families. I expressed my concerns to my mentor Lawrence K. Frank and was intrigued by his description of the traditional extended family in rural America. Multigenerational families consisted of enough adults and children to care for and entertain one another, but the extended family fell apart when individuals moved to the cities to join the industrial work force.

As I prepared to teach a first-year class of landscape architecture graduate students at the University of Pennsylvania, I reflected deeply on how my students and I could contribute to the formation of something akin to extended family living in an urban environment. I realized that the university, located in central Philadelphia, was surrounded by low-income, people-of-color communities—most families headed by mothers who needed support much more than the suburban housewives had. I decided that my students should provide design-and-build services to community self-help projects in the inner city. A variety of government programs made derelict vacant lots available for the kind of projects we envisioned, and, at sites slated for demolition, we found an abundance of potential building material—bricks, marble steps, flagstones from sidewalks.

We wanted to design small open spaces—neighborhood commons—for use by people of different ages all hours of the day and all days of the week. To begin, we would survey people's skills and tools and tailor our designs to the resources available. Growing demand for neighborhood commons inspired the creation of nonprofit corporations that recruited interdisciplinary teams of volunteer professionals who mentored the students and gave continuity to the projects. Primarily middle-class volunteers, eager to invest their energies in meaningful activity, worked hand in hand with neighborhood residents to construct the commons, sponsored by a wide variety of organizations. The names of the community design-and-build service centers changed with their changing focus. We accomplished a lot, and we learned even more, most importantly, that human renewal and the release of creativity and cooperation are more valuable than property improvement and construction of projects.

Outdoor activities on the sidewalks, streets, and vacant lots of North Philadelphia

Melon Neighborhood Commons
The Pilot Project

Philadelphia, Pennsylvania, 1960–62

My graduate students in landscape architecture at the University of Pennsylvania were highly motivated and inspired individuals who had come from all over the world to join the program established by pioneering ecological planner Ian McHarg. They hoped not only to advance their professional careers but also to become better prepared to provide socially meaningful design service. Rather than cater to the conspicuous consumption of clients, they wanted direct contact with communities with real needs.

We began by closely observing how residents of inner-city Philadelphia neighborhoods used open space—how they turned stoops, sidewalks, streets, and vacant lots into extensions of their home territories. These improvised sitting areas, where young and old could talk, play, make music, or just hang

out, nurtured a sense of extended family. Residents revealed a native architectural genius when they added small rooms to buildings as families expanded, making the blocks look like Pueblo architecture. A church initiated the creation of an inner court in their block, and all the residents took down their backyard fences and enjoyed a common yard. Between the buildings they installed segments of the old fencing to protect their commons.

We were also impressed by the energy of the inner-city residents, especially the women, who were very powerful. There was a lot of laughter, which you rarely heard in the white suburbs. Amid heaps of garbage and dilapidated and arsoned buildings, the inner courtyards and vacant lots were full of trees from which young children swung on ropes like Tarzans. They jumped from old cars and played

A city bulldozer cleared rubble from the terrain while neighbors raked it to a smooth surface. We insisted that they retain the existing earth mounds.

Tax-delinquent property was made available by the city for a community playground.

on roofs, leaping from one roof to another. They improvised, transforming junk into imaginative play objects. This chaotic environment provided more opportunities for adventure and fun than the regimented playgrounds designed by social service agencies. Yet seeing children playing dangerously in the streets, in front of fast-moving cars, we realized the urgent need for safe, accessible open space. After a year of reconnaissance, we felt ready for the next step.

One snowy afternoon in North Philadelphia in late 1960, the students and I visited the Friends Neighborhood Guild. As we warmed our freezing hands and feet, executive director Francis Bosworth told us that he might have a project we could help with. The Guild had worked with the City of Philadelphia to pass a bill empowering the city to acquire tax-delinquent properties at sheriff's sales for the cost of the taxes, liens, and interest and then lease them, on a revocable basis, for a dollar a year

to responsible neighborhood organizations. The Guild had secured funding from a private foundation to develop a small play area on twelve lots along Marvine and Melon Streets and Fairmont Avenue. A bulldozer was slated to clear the project area and level the terrain.

The Guild, a white organization, had invited ministers from nearby black churches and representatives from welfare organizations to co-sponsor the project. An advisory council, which included neighborhood block leaders, had been meeting to discuss how to involve other residents, schools, and businessmen in the project. In the spring of 1960, this group had formed the West Poplar Civic League and accepted responsibility for developing and maintaining the lot.

People warned us that the block looked like it had been bombed—twelve vacant lots, twelve empty boarded-up houses, and eleven occupied structures that were unfit for human habitation. Rubble, old

Overview sketch of the commons

Mrs. Bernice Miles, neighborhood leader and mother of twelve, supervised the collection, sorting, cleaning, and stacking of bricks.

furniture, and garbage filled the empty lots, making them an eyesore in the West Poplar area, one of the most neglected sections of North Philadelphia. When we visited the site, however, we saw past the debris to exciting new possibilities. One student imagined all sorts of play spaces created out of existing basements, freestanding walls, and piles of bricks from demolished buildings and suggested that we use timber from the demolitions for climbing structures. The undulating terrain could easily be transformed into steps and retaining walls, which would clearly define different levels of seating and play activity. On some of the mounds, kids could play "King of the Hill."

In the first chill of winter, we took an inventory of the area and discovered that there were many single-mother families. Most of the men, worn down by centuries of racism, were unemployed and hanging around bars. Youth gathered on street corners with few activities to engage their abundant energy. Mothers spoke of parks and playgrounds too far away to be easily accessible to the elderly or to women with small children, and they expressed concern that their children had no safe places to play.

Since North Philadelphia's inner-city residents were primarily African American, I was concerned that my students, most of them Caucasian and from privileged backgrounds, might bring prejudice and misguided assumptions to their encounters with neighborhood residents. We needed to earn the right to serve the community, rather than come in as do-gooders. I hoped that in face-to-face meetings the drama of the residents' lives would move the students to respond with deepening compassion

83

Neighbors and summer work campers from the American Friends Service Committee salvaged, cleaned, and stockpiled bricks and helped lay them for the sandbox, instructed by a neighbor who was a retired mason.

The stigma of squalor can often be easily removed. Scratching the surface we discovered intricate brick pavements covering large areas of what were once the backyards of fashionable buildings.

and respect. I imagined neighborhood residents regaining pride and confidence from their visible accomplishments, becoming creative partners in a design process.

In December 1960, the students met with groups of neighbors in local churches, who made their basements available. Mrs. Bernice Miles, mother of twelve and secretary of the West Poplar Civic League, emerged as the leading spokesperson and organizer. The students listened carefully as residents related the urgencies of their daily lives. As we talked with neighbors, we gradually developed a vision of "Melon Block Commons," a community

space that people of all ages would want to visit and use, a combination sitting area and playground, which would include a sports field and amphitheater for teenagers.

To match our design to available resources and skills, we followed the "principle of the available" and used salvaged materials already on site and from nearby urban renewal demolitions. In human habitat, as in coral reefs, the incremental historical deposits of a place imbue the physical environment with a feeling of timelessness. Residues of former buildings, trees, and landscape features create an air of familiarity. "Historic" building materials bear-

Available building material inspires creative expression. The brick floor of the sandbox, with its intricate circular pattern, was an idea generated and implemented by the children.

This labor of love produced an aesthetically pleasing radial pavement pattern surrounding the circular sandbox.

ing the imprint of use and weather confer a sense of relatedness, which is often sorely lacking in new constructions. This approach was in sharp contrast to the prevailing penchant for brand new construction of virginal structures on landscapes that had been scraped clean. My students had never improvised with salvaged materials. I decided to connect my class with students of environmental design from the Philadelphia College of Art and their instructor William Perry. The students of arts and crafts had a sensuous contact with the materials but were not as sophisticated in assessing spaces. The architecture students contributed a sense of urban space and how to place things in it, while the art students showed them the ingenious things that can be made from salvaged material.

With the arrival of warm weather and student vacations, neighbors and other volunteers were eager to get to work, so, with the assistance of a few professional friends, I incorporated many of the

To salvage marble steps from buildings slated for demolition, we made special arrangements with the Urban Renewal Authority. We bought a pickup truck for the local gang, who became the official scavengers for the project.

We deliberately left in place remnants of a building wall that demolition contractors had not bothered to remove. The students used tiles we found in an abandoned building near the site to embellish the foundation remnants, which became a bench. The colorful designs added a festive ambiance to the commons.

students' ideas into a simpler design. After much discussion the new design met with the approval of the neighborhood. Fortunately, my friend Paul Hogan, a contractor and gifted craftsman, volunteered to coordinate and supervise the construction. We equipped a local teenage gang with an old pickup truck, and they became our "scavengers" of the city's historic building materials, visiting sites slated for demolition to collect marble steps and flagstones from buildings, sidewalks, and backyards. It took four able-bodied young people to lift and carry one marble step. In this experience of interdependence, racial differences became irrelevant; each person was grateful for the other three holding up their part.

The Friends Neighborhood Guild sponsored the participation of twenty-seven young work-campers from the American Friends Service Committee. They joined us for seven weeks, doing strenuous construction work eight hours a day. All the volunteers ate at the worksite and made music together. Small festivals sprang up spontaneously—someone played a guitar and people sang; even the smallest neighborhood children joined in. Local teenagers brought their bongo drums, finding it safer to play on the lot than on the sidewalk. Once I intercepted when police tried to disperse teenagers playing drums on the sidewalk. When I challenged an officer by saying, "Don't touch me and don't talk to me that way," they pushed me into the police car and drove me to the station, unmoved by my explanation that we were building a neighborhood commons. One of our volunteers who taught at the university followed the police wagon in his white convertible Jaguar. When he explained that I was a professor at the university, they released me.

As I had hoped, the salvaged building materials heightened the environmental aesthetic rather than lowered it. The flagstones we had salvaged from demolished sidewalks to create new paved terraces had irregular dimensions, so we filled in the gaps with bricks. The improvised dynamic pattern that resulted manifested "planned indeterminacy," a concept articulated by composer John Cage, which is at the heart of jazz and other forms of modern music and art. In an abandoned building the art students found boxes of mosaic

We invented a simple contraption to hoist the marble steps into place for construction of the amphitheater. Such technology, designed to eliminate backbreaking work, is essential for the well-being of volunteers.

Neighborhood youth and summer work campers constructed the steps for the amphitheater using precision to produce handsome work of high quality.

Young musicians spontaneously found their way to the commons construction site. Their music added an uplifting ambiance as do work songs in indigenous rural cultures. It was a safe place for them to play, unlike the sidewalks where they had run-ins with the police.

The terrace was paved with random-sized flagstones, salvaged from sidewalks. The addition of brick inlay created an interesting and unexpected pattern that demonstrated what one might call an "aesthetic of planned indeterminacy."

tile, which they used to create a colorful design on a retaining wall left over from the demolition of a building.

Our main building materials were those we salvaged from demolition sites. We wanted to use marble steps as seats for the amphitheater, but people expressed concern that they'd be too slippery. Eventually we reached a compromise and agreed to score them to increase traction. The students had designed a big lookout tower that others felt was too dangerous, so we eliminated it. We engaged unemployed men, many of whom were skilled

craftsmen, and because a lot of bricks remained lying around, I looked for and found a retired mason, who taught the students and other volunteers how to construct with brick.

To green the area, we made use of existing ailanthus trees, which grew in profusion in local backyards. Hanson's Nursery donated thirteen large mountain ash trees, and their staff instructed the gang members in digging out the trees and wrapping the ball of soil with burlap. Getting the trees off the truck and into the ground was a big job. Digging out tree pits would have been backbreaking

The familiar marble door-steps enabled the new amphitheater to blend easily into the neighborhood. When Karl saw a group of little girls sweep and then sit on the worn white marble steps, he realized that they had known these steps before.

work as building foundations had been left behind by demolition contractors. So we approached the local telephone company, who dug the pits with their mechanical auger. We received a lot of support from Mayor Richardson Dilworth, who instructed city departments to assist us with heavy equipment and asked the Department of Licenses and Inspections to administer the project.

The phone and electric companies donated poles and cable reels and installed tall poles for the play structures. During construction, children played at the site every day. Observing their spontaneous use of materials and terrain taught us much about playground design. Between the marble steps and the stage we created a large area covered with

wood chips where they played games. The children often asked us whether there would be fences or limited play hours—restraints they had been accustomed to in other play areas. They sighed with relief when we said there would be none. It was wonderful to see these children flowing daily into the emerging spaces, removing their small, fragile bodies from the dangerous streets.

Paul Hogan designed delightful, innovative play equipment, which was inundated with children as soon as it was installed. A constant flow of children climbed up and down the jungle gym, constructed from recycled telephone poles and their crossbars. The slide had had a former life as a galvanized metal tray. Children not only partici-

89

pated in the building of the jungle gym, but added ideas we promptly realized. For a few days our sand circle was so filled with children that we could barely see the sand. Suddenly we realized how very small our new facilities were in comparison to the staggering need.

Neighborhood Renewal Corps

We continued to recruit volunteers from the neighborhood and the city at large, working year round, even during the freezing winter months, adding new play equipment and other amenities to the site as more of the

The phone company supplied and "planted" poles with the help of mechanical augers, which saved much backbreaking labor.

Stopping to ride the horse sometimes caused children to be late to school.

surrounding buildings were demolished. From the initial lots, Melon Commons ultimately encompassed two-thirds of an entire block. The students worked with a commitment that far exceeded school requirements and thought of themselves as a Design Corps. Recognizing their limited time and lack of experience, I recruited volunteer professionals with whom they served apprenticeships.

The successful construction of Melon Commons led to requests for design services by many private and public agencies. As new projects moved out of the design stage into readiness for construction, it became clear that we needed an organizational structure and money for a full-time construction coordinator We established the Neighborhood Renewal Corps (NRC) as an environmental design cadre with a two-fold mission: to provide professional and technical guidance for neighborhood self-help efforts and to mobilize volunteers—professionals, community service work teams, and local youth.

Our first president was Milton Shapp, a politically well-connected electronics entrepreneur who later served twice as governor

of Pennsylvania. He assisted us in establishing a tax-exempt nonprofit corporation in the spring of 1962 and channeled funds to us from his private foundation—about $2,000 a month. Paul Hogan was able to give up his contracting business and work full-time as construction coordinator. We rented a small office and hired a part-time secretary. I became the volunteer executive director, giving up what remained of my private landscape architectural practice to relate the work and concepts of the NRC to the new social legislation coming out of Washington.

Shapp introduced the project to Eunice Shriver, wife of Sargeant Shriver, founding director of the Peace Corps, who considered the NRC a model for a domestic peace corps that took form in 1965 as VISTA (Volunteers in Service to America), now commonly known as AmeriCorps.

We wanted to engage young men in our efforts as the physical construction of neighborhood commons was too strenuous for women and children alone. With the position of adult males in the community weakened by racism and poverty, we believed that working with teenagers would most effectively stimulate community growth. We envisioned the young men who participated in our projects growing in confidence and experience to fill the gap in male leadership. Their vitality, critical judgment, and lack of complacency would bring dynamism to community governance.

We found cable reels in the yards of electric and telephone companies. Much to the delight of youngsters, this reel became a fast-moving merry-go-round. We installed the cable reel on a ball bearing on top of a pipe embedded in concrete.

The students also designed and constructed a sturdier bench from recycled telephone-wiring cross-bars and concrete.

Students from Philadelphia College of Art salvaged concrete cylinders from an operation that tested the strength of cement. They made a plastic mold to form links that joined the cylinders and created a comfortable and aesthetically pleasing bench, which was placed next to the radial brick paving of the sandbox. Unfortunately the bench could not withstand the force released by the pent-up energies of youth.

Neighborhoods are "home turf" to teenagers, just as the family house is home to the smaller child. Unfortunately, in areas like North Philadelphia, street corners are one of the few places where youth can meet. Gathering on sidewalks, they obstruct pedestrian traffic. Playing drums on doorsteps disturbs the peace and brings the police. No wonder they are destructive toward an environment built by others in which they have no place. Youth will be responsible to their community only if they have a vital stake in it. Cities will be safe only if youth experience their neighborhoods as their own—emotionally and spiritually as well as physically.

Neighborhood organizations tend to bring together adults concerned with property and propriety. They reach out to youth but generally do not attract them. Likewise, social service agencies primarily serve women, young children, and seniors and are not effective in inspiring young people. We recognized the potential of youth to be the regenerative energy center of their neighborhood and reached out to teenagers, particularly teenage gangs. When the NRC hired Robert Sickinger, a charismatic theater director who engaged gang members in plays and jazz concerts staged in the commons, the agencies complained that we were trespassing on their domain and advised us to stick to construction and leave the program development to them. After some dialogue, however, they hired my friend Christopher Speeth, who had developed the Philadelphia Children's Theatre. He got youngsters involved in Greek drama—they even built a twenty-foot Trojan horse and put it in Melon Commons.

To add substance to the neighborhood commons movement we wanted to connect with men and women active in emerging civil rights organizations, such as the Congress on Racial Equality (CORE) and the Student Nonviolent Coordinating

Mounds of soil generated races of all kinds. Children created their
own go-cart contraptions. They even liberated a railroad cart.

Committee (SNCC). During the early 1960s, however, CORE was more concerned with securing
opportunities for equal employment than with
improving the physical environment. Although
the SNCC branch in Philadelphia did not end up
participating actively in NRC efforts, the New York
branch spearheaded a neighborhood commons program in Harlem.

Peter Van Dresser, a brilliant city planner,
became a volunteer consultant to the NRC. He had
committed his life to exploring methods to increase
community control through community enterprises,
and after participating in many of our discussions,
Peter prepared a statement on the "Renaissance
of Community." The statement critiqued massive
clearance and reconstruction undertaken in the

name of urban renewal, arguing that the large public expenditures, displacement of masses of people,
and consequent destruction of community life and
traditional values are an unnecessary and unwise
formula. He defined our efforts as the development
of economically and socially self-reliant, small-scale
neighborhood communities.

Peter proposed a partnership approach to
neighborhood restoration—"micro-area" projects,
worked out by NRC architect/planners and landscape architects in collaboration with owner and
tenant committees, designed around small blocks
of land and groupings of structures fronting common but unused backyards. The goal would be
to fully develop the intrinsic virtues of each site
and its existing structures, while also meeting the

Demolition contractors seldom bothered to remove the underground foundations of buildings, so excavating tree pits manually would have been exhausting. To save the volunteers from backbreaking labor, the telephone company dispatched mechanical equipment. The auger, normally used to dig holes for telephone poles, excavated tree pits rapidly.

Hanson's, a local nursery, donated thirteen large ash trees. Their nurserymen instructed and supervised teenaged gang members in balling, burlapping, and hauling the trees to the site. Neighborhood youth, volunteers, and a local Scout troop assisted with unloading and planting.

Parents and others could relax on a paved terrace, shaded by a green canopy of foliage, with an easy view of the sandbox and play areas.

needs of modern urban life by introducing new open-space concepts and community facilities that respected the culture and folkways of new and existing ethnic residents. Designs would utilize locally available and salvaged materials. Additionally, they would be executed by a local labor force and by talent channeled through vocational training, youth opportunity programs, and civic improvement projects. The NRC would pioneer this renaissance of community, enlisting the energies and loyalties of people, especially young people, in ongoing workable enterprises.

In 1962 we ended our relationship with Milton Shapp. He had commissioned a brochure and an article implying that Melon Commons was his idea and failed to give credit to the private and public agencies that had contributed significantly to the project. We realized that Shapp was aimed to use

our collective effort to promote himself and that by funding the operation he felt entitled to make unilateral decisions on important issues.

NRC's next sponsor was the Philadelphia Junior Chamber of Commerce who helped solicit funds, provided a host of technical resources—from legal know-how to scrounging material—and developed good working relationships with municipal and private agencies.

The successful work of the NRC encouraged the City of Philadelphia to develop a citywide Land Utilization Program (LUP) under the Department of Licenses and Inspections. The LUP supplied human resources, equipment, and building material to neighborhood groups in the creation of "vest-pocket" parks. The work of the NRC and the participating neighborhood organizations relieved the city of responsibility for maintaining the der-

At the dedication ceremony for Melon Commons, the City of Philadelphia presented us with an award. This was our first public recognition by the city government.

Poster advertising the talent show.

elict vacant lots on which commons were built. The LUP gradually took over the NRC and focused on constructing mini-parks that contained sitting and play areas. Inspired by the neighborhood commons, they gradually shifted focus from grassroots self-help projects to construction done by city crews. Corporate donors funded some of the LUP projects, and their names appeared on elaborate signs on fences at the parks.

LUP also worked mostly with women to provide safe play space for their children. They did not encourage men and youth from the neighborhood to participate in planning and construction, and thus the males had no stake in caring for and protecting the new parks. I remember seeing women with small children struggling to carry heavy cobblestones while men sat in doorsteps nearby. That level of alienation within the community breeds resentment and the impulse to destroy. Not surprisingly, parks designed and built by paid crews outside the neighborhood, or with no involvement of men or teenagers, are subject to vandalism or neglect.

Throughout the 1960s and 1970s so-called urban renewal projects, accompanied by "redlining"—refusal by banks to loan money for upkeep, repair, and investment in low-income neighborhoods—led to the deterioration of existing housing stock in North Philadelphia, as in many other cities. Absentee landlords, who couldn't get funding for the restoration of their buildings, committed arson on their own properties to collect insurance money. This contributed to the exodus of local residents from the Melon Commons neighborhood.

With fewer people to maintain the Commons it gradually fell into disrepair. Neighbors repeatedly asked the Department of Recreation to help maintain the facilities and to provide planned and organized activities, especially during the summer months, but most of their requests were refused. Eventually neighbors became so disturbed by the loose bricks and broken-down play equipment that they complained to the city, who responded by condemning the Commons and demolishing it.

A political factor contributed to the destruc-

tion of Melon Commons. Mayor Dilworth, who had been very supportive, resigned to run for governor in 1962. In the mid-1960s, the new mayor installed a new director of the Land Utilization Program. Eradicating the evidence of the work the Neighborhood Renewal Corps had accomplished made it possible for her to take all the credit for the vest-pocket parks LUP was constructing. Using the deterioration of the Melon Commons site as an excuse, she ordered the entire commons to be razed.

Sometimes I speculate that if I had stayed in Philadelphia instead of going to other cities to start neighborhood commons corporations, I might have prevented Melon Commons from being destroyed. Since I had cultivated many connections there, I could have applied pressure and rallied supporters to join me in standing in front of the bulldozers.

For many years the entire block remained a vacant asphalt parking lot. Later a high-rise senior citizens' residence was constructed there, surrounded by a tall wrought-iron fence. In the wake of slum clearance, new low-rise housing sprang up around the Melon Commons block. Melon Commons would have provided an ideal recreational setting and a vital meeting place for neighbors to grow community.

Months of planning with local youth culminated in a talent show with spellbinding jazz performances.

The bulldozed lot lay empty for many years.

97

Neighborhood Commons in Perspective

Lessons Learned in the 1960s

1962–69

The idea of creating neighborhood commons on unused land in inner cities captured the imagination of people of all ages and all racial and economic backgrounds. When Lawrence K. Frank visited and observed the construction of Melon Commons, he compared it to the old American tradition of barnraising, which celebrates not only the physical accomplishment of building but also the experience of interdependence and community. We can talk endlessly about building community, but unless people really experience their need for one another it won't develop.

The Neighborhood Renewal Corps (NRC) created six neighborhood commons in Philadelphia before the organization was phased out by the Land Utilization Program (LUP). I recruited volunteer professionals, many from Louis Kahn's office, to lead the design process and mentor my students. Although Kahn's employees enjoyed the unique challenge of working on his designs, they welcomed this opportunity to have contact with clients. One young architect on Kahn's staff, David Rothstein, became so involved with building a commons at the Clara Baldwin Neighborhood House that he cut his employment to half time. The neighbors demonstrated their appreciation when they threw a surprise birthday party for him.

Most commons changed dramatically as time went by. When I revisited the Clara Baldwin Commons in the 1970s, a huge landscape mural

When cars replaced horses, many cement horse troughs, which had been installed by the American Society for Prevention of Cruelty to Animals, were left scattered throughout Philadelphia. David Rothstein discovered one of these and got permission from the city to install it in the Clara Baldwin commons as a fountain, which he accomplished with the help of Paul Hogan and many strong volunteers. The ASPCA was delighted to have us dismantle and recycle the troughs.

Much to the delight of children, the trough was transformed into a gushing fountain in the Clara Baldwin Commons. A local resident who was not involved in the project passed by and exclaimed disparagingly, "We get them once the horses are through with them." Even the most creatively recycled salvaged building material can trigger the resentment of low-income residents who have no choice but to live in shabby environments.

Clara Baldwin (left) was a highly respected community leader who shunned the limelight, but was well known for her extraordinary effectiveness.

Many dilapidated brick buildings around the Clara Baldwin Neighborhood House provided an ample source of materials for the base of the brick and chain-link fence that framed the commons.

dominated the scene. When I visited in 1989, a new high-rise residence for senior citizens, the Clara Baldwin Manor, had been constructed and the neighborhood house had been replaced with a brand new facility, which dispensed social and medical services to the elderly. Returning in 2002 with Paul Hogan, I was disappointed to see the neighborhood house and commons in disrepair. Clara Baldwin's granddaughter, who manages the senior housing, explained that lack of funding had made maintenance impossible but expressed her commitment to restore the center and its commons.

When the trustees of Woodland Presbyterian Church asked the Neighborhood Renewal Corps to install an ivy bed along the sidewalk with a low privet hedge, I saw an opportunity for youth training and employment. I suggested that they create a sidewalk commons for passersby and members of the congregation and persuaded them to use their budget to hire trainees in the Jobs for School Youth program sponsored by the Friends

The Jobs for School Youth participants learned a valuable skill and took pride in their craftsmanship, however, the budget was insufficient to pay them to finish the project, which Karl and the architect completed.

Woodland Church sidewalk commons shortly after its construction in 1962

Neighborhood Guild. Under the guidance of a skilled mason, the young men installed an intricate brick pavement, and beds for trees we planted along the sidewalk. Inspired by the Clara Baldwin commons, we acquired and installed an abandoned horse trough and converted it into a sparkling fountain.

Revisiting Philadelphia in 1989, I observed that the horse trough fountains at Woodland Church and Clara Baldwin commons had been converted to planters.

Horton Block Organization requested help from the NRC to create a commons on a vacant 120-by-60-foot parcel of land, a tax-delinquent property that had been acquired by the city. Thanks to a staggered street system, Horton Street is only one block long and thus safe for children at play. Thirty-seven of the forty surrounding homes were owner occupied, which probably accounted for their

Woodland Church sidewalk commons in 1989. The trees had foliage that made a space for peace and repose.

The Horton Block neighbors worked hard to build a low retaining wall using salvaged marble steps.

cared-for condition. Active participation of adults made the project an authentic self-help effort rooted in the neighborhood. During participatory brainstorming sessions, neighbors suggested that benches, seats, checker tables, a children's game area, and a stage for parties and dances be incorporated in the commons design. The city provided heavy mechanical equipment for clearing and grading the site.

Revisiting NRC work sites in 2002, I saw that only the Woodland Church Commons, our smallest and least ambitious project, had been maintained and improved throughout the years. I was encouraged, however, by the last stop on our field trip at the Village of Arts and Humanities, with its incredible array of public art—colorful murals, mosaic pavements and walls, and sculptural mosaic fence posts and benches. The project, which began by clearing and beautifying an abandoned inner-city lot, has spawned an art and recreation center, community gardens, cottage industries, and a variety of cultural activities. Founder Lily Yeh invited us in during a staff lunch break. The high spirits and lively discussions reminded me of interactions within the NRC forty years earlier.

Inspired by a talk I gave at the Washington Center of Metropolitan Studies in 1962 about the work of the Neighborhood Renewal Corps, a committee formed to bring the concept to Washington, D.C. Three city commissioners backed the committee's efforts. The Center acquired funding and invited me to direct a Neighborhood Commons Program there. I was granted a leave of absence from the University of Pennsylvania.

Revisiting, Karl was pleased that the maturing honey locust trees provided a spatial framework to the commons, but he noted signs of neglect. Visiting the site again in 2002, Paul Hogan and Karl hardly recognized it, encaged by a tall chain-link fence. They were pleased by the ramp for wheelchair access. Paul noted a safety hazard—a tear in the resilient ground cover under the swings.

The Capitol Hill Improvement Committee had contacted the Neighborhood Renewal Corps for advice on self-help construction of simple play structures through creative recycling of salvaged lumber.

I used my experience in Philadelphia to create a more comprehensive program for the Neighborhood Commons Nonprofit Corporation of Washington, D.C. Working closely with planner and architectural historian Frederick Gutheim, who directed the Center of Metropolitan Studies, I recruited members for a board of directors and task committees. Our multiracial board included such prominent community members as Dr. William Nelson, vice president of Howard University, and Robert Nash, president of the National Organization of Minority Architects. We obtained official support from the Washington and Potomac Chapters of the American Society of Landscape Architects, and the American Institute of Architects, who encouraged their members to volunteer. Architects and landscape architects gained valuable experience in community design by serving on the Design Review Committee, which met weekly. Howard University School of Architecture sponsored a Community Design-and-Build Service Education Seminar, and the Homebuilders Association helped with acquisition of building materials. We went through all the necessary channels and procedures to assure that work for Neighborhood Commons would be acknowledged as alternative military service.

I lectured extensively throughout Washington, introducing the idea of neighborhood commons. I initiated a "land-bank" inventory of potential neighborhood commons sites, selected sponsoring agencies, and recommended sites for development. I mobilized social scientists to document and evaluate the program and located volunteer labor, funding, and recycled or low-cost construction materials.

We were approached by Father Geno Baroni, social justice advocate and chaplain of SS. Paul and Augustine Parish House. He wanted to transform the parish house, which had been a convent for more than seventy-five years, into an active neighborhood house. The building was in a densely populated area where the number of young people in trouble

Neighborhood youth helped plant a tree in front of the SS. Paul and Augustine Parish House and rose bushes along the front of the property.

This multipurpose side yard accommodated an outdoor art workshop, which enabled young people to give expression to their imaginings. Their colorful paintings imbued the space with joy.

The other side yard became a basketball court, which was well used. When I revisited in 2002, it had become a parking lot.

with the police was twice as high as the city average. Initially Father Baroni showed me a vacant lot across the street as a potential site for a commons, but I turned him around pointing out that commons for many different purposes could be built on the open spaces surrounding the parish house, which were well protected by a twelve-foot ivy-covered brick wall.

The design was developed by our assistant director, architect Melita Rodeck, in collaboration with architecture students from Howard University. Construction coordinators were two conscientious objectors from the Church of the Brethren who were doing alternative military service. Labor was provided by youngsters from the parish, neighbors, and volunteer teams from the Junior Citizens Corps, Junior Police Corps, and Fellowship House.

We created a brick bench between the steps of the entrance as a gesture of welcome and constructed a finely crafted brick sandbox surrounded by an intricate radial brick pavement in the front yard. Youngsters developed valuable masonry skills as they helped lay the brick patio surface.

Teens expressed a strong desire for a dance floor so the design included an amphitheater in the backyard. Teenagers enthusiastically began to excavate the area, but after a while they ran out of steam. I often found myself continuing the excavation alone or with a couple of volunteers. Using railroad ties to create circular terraced seating, we managed to finish the amphitheater, which in fact was used intensely. I realized, however, that our renderings had been misleading because they didn't express the tremendous amount of effort it would take to make them real.

Revisiting in 1989, I was shocked to find a grass lawn where the amphitheater had been. Much of the structure was below ground level, and I presume it had been filled with dirt and planted over. When I revisited in 2002, much of the brick patio had been dismantled and the remaining brick work needed repair.

If teenagers approached me now with this idea, I would start them out with a temporary plywood floor. If they used it a lot, we could bring some logs to surround it with seating. If the dancing continued, we could bring salvaged boards and connect the logs, adding other rows of logs like an amphitheater. If after a year the dancing had become an established ritual, we could take the boards and use them as forms for concrete. It occurred to me that one should not pour concrete before an activity has cemented itself.

I have fond memories of the elderly residents of the Carrollsburg Public Housing Project, who confided that they didn't feel comfortable in the project's recreation center because it was too formal. They liked our idea of transforming basements surrounding the courtyards into sociability settings, which would be more homelike and easier to access. We helped them convert the basement apartments into places for sewing circles and casual socializing.

One of the great discoveries in our land bank survey was a unique 10,000-square-foot lot surrounded by inner-block public alleys that bordered the backyards of the residents, making access to the lot very easy. The neighborhood residents had thought all along that the land belonged to an absentee landlord, but it was actually an undeveloped and forgotten part of a 1930s effort to build small-scale decentralized playgrounds.

When neighbors learned that the lot was city-owned, they were eager to develop a commons and offered their organization, Neighbors Inc., as the sponsoring agency. The group had formed during the late 1950s to discourage the exodus of white families to the suburbs. These racially mixed neighbors participated actively in the design and even offered a prize for the best schemes. Volunteer professional designers with Neighborhood Commons presented their plans for comments and discussion. Residents participated actively in the construction of the commons and suggested that the terraced patios be surfaced with individualized concrete pavement blocks they made themselves. The commons was composed of an upper level with benches and tables for sitting, talking, and supervising children at play and a lower level with a barbecue for cookouts and multifamily gatherings. In 2002 I was sad to find the lot uncared-for, unused, and enclosed by an ugly chain-link fence.

Eastland Gardens, the one commons we built in D.C. that was moderately well preserved, is under the jurisdiction of the National Park Service, who maintain it, but it did not appear to be well used. In retrospect I realized that our preoccupation with design and construction left little time and energy for nurturing an ongoing sense of community among the neighborhood residents who would use the commons.

In early 1963 architect George Kostritsky asked me to help him start a neighborhood commons nonprofit corporation in Baltimore, Maryland. Architect M. J. Brodie of the Baltimore Urban Renewal and Housing Agency (BURHA) was enthusiastic about the idea and arranged for me

The welcoming brick bench between the steps of the entrance in 1989. The tree we had planted 27 years earlier had grown a lot.

Revisiting in 2002, Karl was delighted that the bench had survived forty years of use. The tree behind the bench had apparently outgrown its bed. In its place was a Peace Pole, similar to the one we planted in the Peralta Garden Commons in Berkeley.

105

to make presentations to city officials and agencies. The Junior League of Baltimore decided to sponsor the program, and Mayor Thomas J. D'Alesandro, III, joined the board of directors. At the request of homeowners in a black middle-class neighborhood in West Baltimore, we developed a design for Elgin Commons, which included a tot lot, horseshoes, and a basketball court. Unfortunately, there was not enough ongoing commitment and volunteer labor to complete the project.

I was excited to learn that a number of Baltimore neighborhoods had city-owned open spaces at the center of each block, which seemed ideal for creating inner-block commons. No such commons were built, however, probably because we failed to connect with community leaders who could generate support for the idea. Although the city developed many of these inner-block open spaces with input from surrounding residents, too many were poorly maintained and became a milieu for drug dealing.

Although the Neighborhood Commons organization in Baltimore only existed for two years, it created fertile ground for the emergence in 1968 of the Neighborhood Design Center, which links volunteer professionals with community projects in low-income neighborhoods and assists over one hundred community-sponsored projects each year.

In response to growing interest and inquiries about our work, I visited various cities, giving lectures, looking at potential project sites, and helping start new community design centers. Some people familiar with my work in Philadelphia and Washington, D.C. asserted that those projects could not be replicated because I was doing the work of three people. They were proved wrong, as a broad range of people and organizations in different cities sponsored and carried out the work. About fifty neighborhood commons were built during the 1960s and 1970s guided by design review committees of the various organizations.

With the Neighborhood Commons Nonprofit Corporation of New York City, formed in late 1963, emphasis shifted from designing and building spaces to empowering a community. In Philadelphia I had begun a lifelong friendship with Carl Anthony, a teenager attending programs at Heritage House, a vibrant black cultural center that supported our work. Carl was fascinated with the creation of Melon Commons and its relationship to the surrounding community, and we often walked through the neighborhood sharing observations. When Carl moved to New York to study architecture at Columbia University, he worked at the Harlem Education Project (HEP), a program of the Northern Student Movement Coordinating Committee for Civil Rights (NSM). Carl and his colleagues saw the neighborhood commons as a way of materializing Martin Luther King, Jr.'s dream of human equality and dignity. Providing opportunities for youth to make a tangible contribution to themselves and their neighborhoods while exposing them to architecture, horticulture, photography, masonry, carpentry, and landscape gardening could compensate for a restrictive overemphasis on written and verbal learning in their classrooms.

Carl invited me to explore the development of a neighborhood commons in Harlem, and I made special trips to New York to attend HEP workshops and meetings, offering what counsel I could. In the course of our discussions NSM endorsed Neighborhood Commons as a national program to supplement their already established tutorials. HEP volunteers worked with neighborhood residents to plan community activities—summer tutoring, weekend work parties, neighborhood festivals, and job training for unemployed youth. They prepared a list of skilled volunteers and shared ideas for the use of a commons.

In the spring of 1964 neighborhood residents came out en masse for a block party to celebrate the inauguration of a neighborhood commons project, on a city-owned lot on West 147th Street. The *Harlem Voice* covered the event, which expressed the massive response to emerging black leadership. Carl Anthony spoke about community energy as an idea whose time had come, and a young student fresh from civil rights actions in the South led the crowd in freedom songs ending with "We Shall Overcome." At subsequent work parties they enthusiastically cleared out the garbage-filled lot, filling endless truckloads with debris, which the city sanitation department refused to haul away.

Unfortunately exhaustion set in before construction could begin. The three well-intentioned young white volunteer architects that Carl recruited produced an overly complex design, including a basketball court, a bowling area, and a monumental barbecue pit, which kept the residents and volunteers endlessly digging trenches for foundations. The long, hard clean-up effort, heavy construction work, and the difficulty of obtaining materials and transporting them to the site led to burnout, and the construction was not completed. Later we realized that we should have started with a much simpler design. For example, we could have used a steel drum cut in half as a barbecue at the end of the first day's work, in an immediate celebration of the magnificent investment of voluntary energy.

The Spirit of the Commons

We were so deeply absorbed in the planning, design, and building of neighborhood commons that we did not dwell enough on awakening the spirit of the commons in people's minds and hearts. Many neighborhood commons were not adequately maintained because of people's failure to bond with one another around a shared vision of being in community. Reverend William Baxter of St. Mark's Episcopal Church on Capitol Hill gave

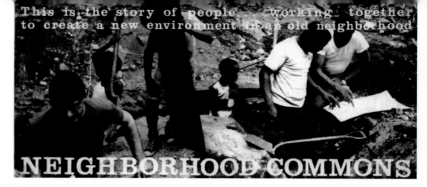

Outreach brochure for the neighborhood commons project in Harlem.

invaluable counsel on the development of neighborhood commons, which is still pertinent today. After losing his church building to the expansion of the Capitol, he focused on the significance of a church without walls. He questioned our reliance on the built commons to nurture community life. In a letter to me in 1963 he wrote of

> the need for a deeper ground than the ground of the Commons … in order to sustain the frail though wonderful concern for one's neighbors through the periods of inevitable disappointment when plans fall through, expected entertainment doesn't materialize, and neighbor fights neighbor over some inconsequential slight that has grown up into great importance between them.

Of all the projects I was involved in, the one that most deeply actualized the spirit of the commons was in Chicago. Ron Engel and Neil Shadle, Unitarian Universalist ministers and faculty members at the Meadville Theological School of Lombard College in Chicago, were inspired by Rev. Baxter's insights. They invited me to help establish a commons there in the spring of 1965 as a memorial to our mutual friend James Reeb, a Unitarian Universalist minister murdered in Selma, Alabama, after marching with Dr. Martin Luther King. Ron and Neil were operating the Unitarian Universalist Center for Urban Ministry in a second-floor office above a tavern in the struggling Lincoln Park

The Neighborhood Commons storefront in North Chicago

neighborhood of North Chicago. They asked their student interns to choose a particular area of concern—politics, education, housing, or civil rights—and expected them to become full partners in the group ministry. They were joined by lay volunteers from congregations in nearby suburbs who hoped to serve as a channel of information and expertise to inner-city residents whose personal and family crises were not being addressed by any public or private agencies.

When I arrived, they were devoting themselves to tracking down slum landlords and pressuring them to observe building codes. I suggested that they could serve more effectively as inspirers than as protesters and recommended that they transform their headquarters from a center of protest to a center of promise. They had also invited my friend Milton Kotler to participate in discussions envisioning a neighborhood commons. Milton, a fellow of the Institute of Policy Studies and author of the book *Neighborhood Government,* was later instrumental in founding the National Association of Neighborhoods. He considered neighborhood commons and neighborhood development corporations as a first step toward grassroots democracy.

The headquarters of the Center for Urban Ministry gradually became a commons, organized as the Neighborhood Commons Corporation of Chicago (NCC), a nonprofit, tax-exempt corporation run by a board of neighborhood members. The mission of the NCC was primarily to conduct a listening and enabling ministry that would nurture the potential for communal response and promote social and political awareness and change. The founders hoped that as a formal corporate entity the NCC might become a vehicle for various community development projects, especially low-income housing. Richard Brown, a neighborhood resident and member of the Congress on Racial Equality (CORE), played an essential role in developing the NCC, representing the African American community neighborhood, networking with community agencies, leading various NCC projects, and working with local youth. In March 1966 the NCC employed Dick as a full-time staff person and lay minister.

According to Ron, the Commons was "a fellowship of men and women who came together with the shared goal of bringing justice to the world." In June 1966 at least a dozen members went to Mississippi to march in support of James Meredith. The racially and culturally diverse group was eager to collaborate on community development projects.

The community around North and Clybourn faced an array of problems—the displacement of low-income and welfare residents by Chicago's second major urban renewal project, poor and unresponsive neighborhood schools, along with the usual problems of drug addiction, alcoholism, prostitution, exploitation by landlords, inflated food prices, police harassment, and lack of political power. Ron, Neil, and Richard decided to focus on public education and affordable housing. Ron began organizing parents of children in the local elementary school, and Neil worked on enabling the NCC to purchase and maintain low-income housing, establishing it as a black-run housing corporation that still exists today. Drawing upon many of the same local board

MID-CITY COMMUNICATOR

Masthead and clippings from the Mid-City Community Congress newsletter

VOLUME 1, NUMBER 10   MID-CITY COMMUNITY CONGRESS, INC.   JULY 21, 1967

members, Neil also formed the Neighborhood Development Corporation, which explored community-operated business ventures, for a time running a clothing outlet store for low-income families.

The NCC and the NDC moved their operations to a larger and more accessible storefront in one of the NCC's own buildings, providing space for an office, a Saturday morning music school taught by suburban volunteers, and meeting rooms for the Mulligan School PTA, the Sheffield Avenue Co-op Buying Club, and local campaigns such as a school boycott. The experience of developing community-run housing inspired the NCC to begin a low-income housing project on land made available by urban renewal, a project completed a few years later. They envisioned additional projects—a daycare center, restaurant, co-op savings and loan, continuing education in democratic citizenship, co-operative projects with local artists, and expanded performing-arts education for children.

As the black power movement spread among neighborhood residents, economic empowerment for black residents became the central concern. The vision of a racially diverse community faded as resentment against whites and conflicts between black and Latino residents intensified. Ron and Neil's recommendation that the NCC director's contract not be renewed was interpreted as racial

prejudice. In response to a black protest, Ron and Neil stepped down, and Meadville/Lombard Theological School negotiated a new relationship with the NCC, enabling the black-owned cooperative housing project to continue. Surviving gentrification, it exists today as one of the few racially and class-inclusive communities on Chicago's north side.

In 1966 I lectured at Webster College, just outside St. Louis, Missouri, and conducted workshops in the art department, guiding students in transforming an existing space into a temporary student-faculty commons. The students were eager to contribute to social transformation on their campus. While there, I was introduced to social studies professor V. Miller Newton, founder of the Mid-City Community Congress, an interracial inner-city revitalization organization. With support from the St. Louis Redevelopment Authority, a city-sponsored nonprofit, Newton engaged five Webster undergrads in a summer internship—living in the black community near Gaslight Square and working with neighbors to envision and design five commons. The students, who had taken courses with Newton, were dedicated to the civil rights movement. Two art students, Terry Barrett and John Traversa, former seminarians, had worked with me at Webster and were selected to coordinate the building of the commons.

Unfortunately Webster offered no indus-

A Neighborhood Commons is children sitting in three tons of sand and liking it.

A Neighborhood Commons is Mr. Drake bringing bricks and building a barbecue pit.

A Neighborhood Commons is lugging railroad ties.

A Neighborhood Commons is 20 carpenters building one table.

The workshop at the Landscape Technician Training Program was an accumulator of creative energy.

In the creative environment of the workshop center one of the students revealed great talent in painting.

The workshop functioned as a showroom for outdoor furniture built by the students.

The sculptures the students made with salvaged wood were sold in a local gallery.

trial design or architecture courses—the artists were imaginative but lacked construction savvy. Inspired by photos of play equipment fashioned from old telephone poles, they had neither tools nor skills to utilize the ones the phone company unloaded on an informal baseball diamond, making it unusable by neighborhood youth. Another overly ambitious project backfired when the coordinators found themselves with insufficient skills and manpower to spread donated asphalt evenly for creating a basketball half-court in a vacant lot. Although neighbors reassured them that they preferred parking on lumpy asphalt to parking on dirt, the students were frustrated by this failure and discouraged by their inability to complete any of the commons by summer's end.

Centers That Function as Commons

Neighborhood commons building inevitably came to a halt during the snowy East Coast winters. We addressed this problem in 1967 in Columbus, Ohio, by creating a design-and-construction center in an industrial building, which became the headquarters of the Columbus Urban Environmental Workshop (CUE). Architect Mark Feinknopf was teaching at Ohio State University and joined the Junior Chamber of Commerce where he met other idealistic and energetic young professionals, who were looking for ways to contribute to solving social problems. Mark was familiar with the work my students and I had done in Philadelphia and introduced it to his colleagues and to Columbus's Director of Development, James Crozier. Sponsored by the Junior Chamber and the American Institute of Architects, CUE became a bridge between volunteer professionals, city government, the university, and inner-city communities.

The center, located between a low-income residential neighborhood and the city business district, became a gathering place for people of differing ages and backgrounds to work creatively—sharing hopes and concerns and freely experimenting with ideas and building materials. Volunteer professionals provided services to community groups. Over

Participants experienced creativity and community in the workshop of the Bread and Puppet Theater summer program.

time, equipment and tools accumulated and the workshop center became a depot for salvageable building materials and a showroom for ingeniously created objects. Neighborhood residents, artists, and volunteer professionals explored the production of outdoor furnishings, pavement blocks, and sections of trellis, arbors, and fences that could easily be assembled outdoors with the coming of spring.

Having a year-round meeting place strengthened community ties and provided opportunities for organizational development. Helping plan Columbus's Model Cities Program, CUE proposed the construction of a Neighborhood Forum in each of six districts—a combination of outdoor space and indoor center.

A few years earlier, in 1964, I had participated in the creation of a workshop center in Washington, D.C. The Landscape Technician Training Program, located in an old firemen's training station, was conducted by the Neighborhood Commons Corporation and funded by the U.S. Department of Labor with support from the landscape industry and its professional and trade organizations.

Fifty school dropouts, aged nineteen to twenty-one, were trained in landscaping, masonry, carpentry, and welding. They worked weekends restoring residential landscapes on Capitol Hill. In the workshop, inspired by a gifted staff member, students began to make sculptures out of salvaged building materials, and their work was sold by a local gallery. One student revealed great talent as a painter and received a scholarship to a prestigious art school.

Students also created prefabricated outdoor furnishings as prototypes for small industry. My mentor Louis Kahn called such centers sanctuaries for experimentation.

In the summer of 1966, I was involved in another inspiring, although temporary, workshop center. My friend Shirley Chesney, who was also a member of New York City's Parks and Playgrounds Council, collaborated with me on a summer youth program funded by the Parks Department. It was aimed at reducing crime in the parks by creating activities for youth. We engaged Peter Schumann, founder and director of the Bread and Puppet Theater, to conduct a workshop in the South Bronx, guiding youth in creating huge puppets and developing a street theater production, "The Sky Is Falling," which they performed in all of New York's five boroughs.

Although the term "center" usually implies a tangible building, creative communication and action is at the heart of it. One can distinguish several levels of such concentrated creative energy—an individual whose charisma and creativity engages and empowers people creates a human energy center without walls. The comfortable spaces of people who open their living rooms or backyards for collaborative creative efforts function as "home base"

Neighborhood youth dramatized their own reality, creating huge puppets to portray slumlords for "The Sky is Falling," a street theater production.

111

Peter Schumann took the youth to a clay pit in New Jersey to get the clay for a big crocodile head, which they attached to an extremely long colorful fabric body carried by a hundred youngsters.

centers. Community garden commons and small-scale community resource centers function as extensions of home territory. Larger community centers, provided by churches, agencies, or city government, can marshal greater resources, but they risk stifling creativity by focusing too much on administrative structure. I often recall E. F. Schumacher's dictum, "Small Is Beautiful."

After the first year CUE kept expanding its volunteer base and its projects. The founding core of volunteers were overwhelmed by the enormous need. When a full-time manager was hired after the second year, the tight-knit team spirit that had made the organization so dynamic began to wane. The young professionals at the core of the organization found themselves needing to invest more time and energy in their careers and families. Rather than fundraising to hire more staff, they decided to dissolve the organization. Still CUE volunteers continued to collaborate with one another and to work with community groups. Their friendships have endured, and some of their projects, such as a concert in the park series, are ongoing. In 1982 Mark Feinknopf helped found the Neighborhood Design Center at Ohio State's School of Architecture to provide affordable design and planning services to central-city neighborhoods.

In 1967 I consulted with students and faculty at the University of Syracuse after helping them develop a proposal for a national competition funded by the Pittsburgh Plate Glass Foundation. Our proposal for a one-year program where students of architec-

ture and landscape architecture would work with staff and neighbors to create a commons in a neighborhood was the winner. I worked with several professors and the Syracuse Planning Department to set up the Neighborhood Environment Program (NEP). Many students, who were involved in the student empowerment movement that was sweeping through U.S. colleges and universities, supported the work of the NEP, inspired by the idea that they could contribute to social and environmental betterment.

Students conducted a study of a low-income neighborhood, suggesting possible improvements in housing and open space. They also designed play equipment and outdoor furnishing components that could be easily assembled and rearranged to meet changing needs. As in many student-based projects, there was too little involvement with community residents. Both students and neighbors complained that the community liaison/coordinator I had hired looked down on their ideas, which discouraged them. The most successful project was the conversion of a former barbershop into a teen center. The students drew up plans, and the teens selected those they liked best.

Reflections on Urban Open Space

In 1968 I received a generous creative development grant from the van Ameringen Foundation, who specialize in improving mental health in underserved communities. The grant, which was administered by the Massachusetts Institute of Technology (MIT) where I began to teach, made it possible for me to revisit and document many of the neighborhood commons sites I had worked on and other small urban open-space projects implemented through standard contract work, youth and employment development programs, and self-help efforts. I was assisted by photographer Nanine Clay Greene.

The Kerner Commission study on the causes of the 1967 urban riots determined that lack of open space and recreation facilities and programs was the fifth most pressing grievance of those involved in the riots. We observed that neighborhood open-space development expands opportunities for skill building, employment, small business enterprise, and self-help neighborhood initiatives. It allows citizens to take immediate short-range actions that improve their quality of life and prepares them for participation in long-range planning. At the same time, our survey revealed that hundreds of new urban playgrounds, plazas, tot-lots, greenways, and small parks were being built with little or no communication among designers, builders, and users—even within the same city. People were imitating finished projects described in official reports without understanding the problems and pitfalls. We recommended establishing a national neighborhood open space program as a clearinghouse for information exchange and networking. Satellite centers, ideally connected to schools of environmental design, would reach more communities.

Our research culminated in a conference/workshop on urban open space in Washington, D.C. in March 1969. Rather than investing the balance of my grant to publish a book on my neighborhood commons work, I chose to create a conference for all the significant players involved in the creation of neighborhood commons: (1) neighborhood residents and organizers—the experts on what is best for their environment, (2) students, educators, and researchers, (3) volunteer professionals—planners, architects, landscape architects, and others, (4) representatives of nonprofit organizations, and (5) representatives of municipal, state, and federal agencies. Bringing together divergent interest groups seemed urgent in light of growing racial and socio-economic tensions. Usually only professionals can afford to attend conferences, but a grant from the American Society of Landscape Architects (ASLA) Foundation paid neighborhood residents—teenagers and adults—to participate in the conference and covered their transportation and lodging.

I was confident that the conference would provide a state-of-the-art account of the work and advance the field through the interaction of the participants. Instead of preconceiving specific topics, we anticipated that the interactions and encounters among the participants would generate insightful discussions. It would be an Encounter Forum where participants would meet in three different groupings: (1) those with similar roles, but from different cities, (2) by lot in mixed groups with equal distribution of roles, (3) all the representatives from one city. On the last day we wanted to provide an arena for the exponents of various points of view, who were willing to speak in front of the entire assembly.

All participants assembled for the five-hour closing session during which strong recommendations were made for democratizing landscape architecture.

A session of the Workshop on Urban Open Space in 1969, sponsored by the American Society of Landscape Architects (ASLA)

workshop on urban open space

The U.S. Department of Housing and Urban Development (HUD) funded the production of a booklet summarizing the conference proceedings. It was welcomed by many as the first publication to provide information and guidelines for participatory urban open space projects.

About 140 people participated in the conference, over half of whom I had personally invited. We exchanged experiences, paved the way for future dialogues, and envisioned what our next steps might be. I appreciated how difficult it was, especially for people of color, to remain open and resist racial polarization. Valuable observations and recommendations emerged from the gathering:

- Federal and local governments should make more funds available for urban open space development and follow up with additional funding for recreation programs and site maintenance and repair.
- We need a Congressional lobby for open space to promote its value and press for innovation and excellence.
- Nonprofit agencies and foundations can support innovative programs through their experimental phase. Problems arise when they impose too many requirements and restrictions, withdraw funds prematurely, or fail to communicate effectively with neighborhood residents, professional designers, and city departments who will provide long-term funding.
- The process is more important than the con-

structed project. Neighborhood commons need to have full participation by all potential users, especially teenagers.

- Most small-scale inner-city recreation areas failed because neighborhood residents, the ultimate users of these open spaces, were not sufficiently engaged in their design and construction.
- Since many grassroots leaders have developed a level of competence in inner-city neighborhood development that outmatches that of so-called professionals, the ASLA should establish a division of inner-city practice and an adjunct "Neighborhood Resident Advisory Committee."
- Designers and planners should recognize the community as their client and the neighborhood professional as their consultant or partner.
- Schools of planning, architecture, and landscape architecture should recruit inner-city youth so they can be trained to work effectively on their own turf. Academic requirements should be waived for people with extensive experience and leadership ability and credit given for community organizing and park/playground development.

The annual Christmas party at the Court of Ideas in Pittsburgh

Another annual event at the Court of Ideas —the Spring Thing

I appreciated the support of ASLA president Theodore Osmundson and other ASLA members, who expressed their commitment to broaden the base of landscape architectural service to include inner-city neighborhoods.

Looking back I realize that by moving frequently to introduce the concept of neighborhood commons in new cities, I failed to provide ongoing support and guidance that projects needed to root themselves in the community. One of the most successful neighborhood revitalization projects I encountered during our survey was the Court of Ideas in Pittsburgh, Pennsylvania. The originator, architect Troy West, who was teaching at Carnegie Melon University, joined the Citizens' Committee for Hill District Renewal in 1965, drawn by the vibrant culture of the primarily black residents. There he encountered Ed Ellis, a powerful black man who was working with local youth. Ed became the neighborhood professional who tutored Troy and his students and guided them in their desire to serve the community. Troy's students collaborated with youth in Ed's program to restore a storefront and adjacent buildings, create an outdoor commons, and sponsor cultural activities. After winning the first *Progressive Architecture* award ever given to a citizen-based project, they received funding from the Office of Economic Opportunity for a youth drug-rehabilitation program based on architecture.

University students and neighborhood youth worked together to renovate local substandard housing. The program expanded as they forged collaborations with businesses and nonprofits, including the Federated Garden Clubs with whom I had worked for many years. With the advent of the Nixon administration funding began to dwindle, and the program ended in 1973 when Troy, who became a lifelong friend, lost his teaching position and moved to Newark to join the faculty of the new school of architecture at New Jersey Institute of Technology.

In retrospect I wish that we had begun more slowly and humbly to test the ground before producing designs and starting construction. We did not recognize how much we needed city departments to help with heavy work, resources, and maintenance, and how much time and effort it would take to establish relationships of trust and collaboration with them and maintain those connections throughout changing administrations. Despite our naiveté and inability to actualize and maintain much of what we envisioned, we shared a tremendous eagerness to create spaces where people could come together and experience a sense of community on a neighborhood block level. We brought that idealism and enthusiasm into our subsequent work.

After the lawn was established, one of the students who served as volunteer caretakers mowed the grass to spell the word "PEACE."

Campus-Neighborhood Peace Garden and Campus Commons

Massachusetts College of Art, Boston, 1970

One day in Boston I was moved by the sight of a long line of people in black cloaks and white masks walking through town. When I spoke with them I learned that they were students at Massachusetts College of Art (MCA). Their highly effective performance impressed me as they demonstrated their opposition to the Vietnam War and mobilized onlookers to support the protest. In the course of our conversation they invited me to visit the college and asked if I could suggest how they might celebrate the first Earth Day, fast approaching.

Surveying the college grounds in Brookline, a busy section of Boston close to Children's Hospital, I noted the lack of open spaces both on the campus and in the surrounding neighborhood. I suggested that the students transform a large empty hardpan parking lot into a Campus-Neighborhood Peace Garden. The project excited the students, and many

Overview of patio paving

The students were enthusiastic about reclaiming the compacted soil and creating a garden.

The students created a patio, arranging recycled bricks in an intricate pattern.

volunteers showed up to dig and aerate the soil and plant a garden. They installed a lawn and surrounded it with beds of colorful flowers. The garden became a green oasis, a tangible symbol of transformation, where students and neighborhood residents could meet face to face in a shared space. Much to our delight the letters P E A C E appeared in the lawn after a student ingeniously carved them from the grass while mowing.

One day a young man drove up in an expensive sports car and asked to talk with me. "Look," he said, "I just came from Children's Hospital across the street and the doctor told me that my girlfriend, who was in a motorbike accident with me, is still in a coma and will not make it. Can I plant a flower for her in your garden?" It was a touching experience. Later, some patients and staff in the hospital across the street told us how much they enjoyed looking at the garden. "Don't put up

Students were happy to volunteer for garden maintenance.

Students refurbish an old print shop to create a student-faculty commons.

a hedge," they pleaded, "we want to see the garden. It's the only green thing in view." So the garden became a neighborhood commons, and gradually I realized that the peace garden had great significance for people living in the area.

Faculty members supported the project and welcomed the idea of bringing a social dimension to the practice of art. After I made some presentations to the faculty, the president of the college invited me to develop a new division of community design-and-build service. After much soul searching I accepted the invitation and gave up my tenure track at MIT to start the Department of Environmental Arts at MCA. It was a risky move, but the challenge of starting a full-fledged community design-and-build service program intrigued me. I hired two architect friends, David Dobereiner and Jan Wampler, as lecturers and continued to work half time at MIT to make our budget stretch. I felt much more at home in the company of artists and art students than with some of my fellow MIT faculty members, who were very competitive and driven by ambition.

First we created a lively workshop space for students, surrounded by windows and adjacent to the peace garden. Jan Wampler worked with students to create a greenhouse accessible from the workshop and facing the garden. David helped the students create modular units so that they could personalize their study spaces and created a second floor loft where students could hang out.

Fellow faculty member Lowry Burgess helped create the student-faculty commons.
One of the last steps was to place a potted plant at the center of each table.

He also guided them in transforming the alienating cafeteria room into a welcoming place.

I involved students and faculty in converting a filthy unused print shop into a student-faculty commons. We installed a cork floor, furnished the room with comfortable foam-rubber seating and wooden tables handcrafted by students, and filled the space with hanging plants. Students and faculty gathered there to discuss the future of the college, which was about to expand into new facilities. The program focused effectively on in-house service and successfully transformed and created new spaces on campus.

At a meeting with the seven division heads, the MCA president announced that he would like to democratize the institution by having these seven take management of the school. I was surprised when he later changed direction and decided to shift resources from the Environmental Arts program to a Department of Architectural Design focused on providing a career boost to underprivileged local youth, preparing them for graduate work in architecture. After my departure he asked for my recommendation of someone to head this new program, and I suggested David Dobereiner, who accepted the position.

David Dobereiner designed a system of pre-fabricated components to create modular individual spaces for the painting students.

The student-built loft expanded the possibilities for interaction and collaboration.

View of the greenhouse from the peace garden

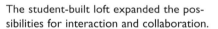

The lot at the corner of Murray and Brunswick before construction of the commons

Neighborhood organizations and Pueblo City families received keys to the commons, which was used for special events and quiet family gatherings. The rear of the lot was devoted to community gardening.

Pueblo City Commons Cluster

Constructing Commons in Long-term Subsidized Housing

Newark, New Jersey, 1978

On the advice of my friend Troy West, I applied for a teaching position at the new School of Architecture at New Jersey Institute of Technology (NJIT) in Newark. In 1977, I was delighted to accept a position of associate professor there. All my earlier work had prepared me to take on Newark, still dominated by evidence of the race riots that had left behind residential areas full of vacant lots cleared of burned-down buildings. Rather than viewing the abundance of vacant lots as a detriment, I saw the possibility of using this available land to cultivate community gardens and market farming. I wrote an article called "Newark: the Garden City of the Garden State," which the local chamber of commerce published in its magazine.

As I developed a community design-and-build service education program at NJIT, I spent quite a few years working with residents of low-income people-of-color neighborhoods and staff of public and private agencies involved in participatory planning and design. Among other projects, my students designed a master open-space plan for the Westside Development Corporation and a commons for the Tri-City Neighborhood organization featuring play equipment and a fence that served as an outdoor easel. They also designed a place of worship for a

The retaining wall in this commons on Brunswick and Astor doubled as a bench. Residents used the planting bed to grow food and flowers. We planted trees along the street to help define the space.

We installed a sandbox in each of the outdoor commons.

With minimal or no maintenance, the retaining walls, sandbox, and woodchip paths all decomposed with the passage of time, but the mature trees continued to serve their intended function of defining the space.

senior housing project and the courtyard for the Department of Parks and Recreation, and created a temporary Japanese Pavilion for the annual Branch Brook Park Cherry Blossom Festival.

I became friends with developer Sanford Gallanter, also a lawyer and certified public accountant, and his wife Linda, an educator. Sanford was born and raised in Newark and participated actively in a campaign to elect its first black mayor. We had a lot of talks about the importance of access to usable open space near housing so that people could get to know each other and develop a sense of community, thus creating a safer neighborhood. His business, The Aspen Corporation (TAC), took advantage of a U.S. Department of Housing and Urban Development (HUD) program that financed the restoration and rehabilitation of abandoned but physically sound dwellings to create affordable housing in Newark's Lincoln Park neighborhood. Sanford hired me to design and supervise the construction of five commons to serve the residents of buildings he had restored in a cluster called Pueblo City, which had a total of eighty-six subsidized units. I was very happy

The commons in the rear of 68–74 Astor was very popular for playing ball.

to participate in this project, administered through HUD's Section 8 housing program, as it would help protect tenants from the displacing effect of gentrification for the duration of the buildings' thirty-year mortgage. Sanford also made available a vacant lot across the street, at the corner of Murray and Brunswick, as a central commons where residents of the housing complex could interact with the surrounding community. He was so pleased with the Pueblo City Commons that he hired me to install community garden commons in a number of other properties undergoing renovations by TAC.

Before developing the design for the commons, I met extensively with long-time neighborhood residents, such as Charles Mullin and Mrs. Anderson, both ardent gardeners living nearby, who had been gardening on part of the lot at Murray and Brunswick for years, planting and caring for tulips and other bulbs in spring and a series of annual flowers during the summer and fall. They also decorated the garden during the Christmas holidays. I surveyed all the existing vegetation, topography, and structures surrounding the sites and then designed the spaces for optimum flexibility of use and maximum participation of users. Whether a particular area became a lawn or a vegetable or flower garden depended on the choices of future tenants and might change from year to year.

We constructed retaining walls, which also functioned as benches, from railroad ties and heavy timber planks recycled from housing

The elevated patio doubled as a place for play and for cultural events. The steps provided a great sociability setting.

The retaining wall–benches, made of railroad ties and salvaged lumber, defined spaces for gatherings, like this meeting of Troy West and his students.

The commons at the rear of 46–52 Astor

demolition. They would help prevent erosion and compaction of soil on the sloping terrain. We then covered all other surfaces with plantings or a wood chip mulch and planted trees to create a strong spatial framework. Raised planting beds, designed to frame the commons and integrate the terrain of the surrounding properties, made gardening more convenient for seniors and residents with limited mobility.

Since the construction crew consisted of men who had little or no experience in landscape construction, I trained and supervised them. We used bulldozers to grade the terrain, and the crew spread topsoil on all the planting areas. Neighborhood men were often hired into the construction force, which added another element of community involvement to the project. Landscape contractors, selected through competitive bidding, planted trees and shrubs and spread woodchips.

An elevated patio in the commons behind 68–74 Astor and a free-standing wooden deck in the commons behind 20–30 Astor served as stages for cultural events and for children's spontaneous play. We installed

When Karl revisited in the 1990s, the deck, lawn, raised bed, and fence had all decomposed or fallen into disrepair.

A wooden deck constructed in the commons at the rear of 20–30 Astor

a sandbox in each of the commons, anticipating that the Trust for Public Land and other such organizations would provide more elaborate play equipment such as swings, slides, and other play structures in all the open-space commons except in the central one at Murray and Brunswick, designed for neighborhood gatherings and quiet family use. Later I succeeded in obtaining picnic tables, barbecues made from halved steel drums, and a basketball stanchion and net from the Trust for Public Land. We had a ceremonial dedication and tour of the Pueblo City buildings on June 26, 1978.

Once people moved in and formed a resident council, I brought in my students to assist the residents in envisioning and constructing outdoor furnishings and play equipment for the various commons. I realized that we needed a space in which neighbors could review student-generated designs, since it would be awkward and inconvenient for the residents to come to the university. With a grant from the Victoria Foundation and ongoing funding from NJIT we created a satellite university-community design-and-construction workshop in the basement of St. Luke AME Church across the street from the central commons. There students could build trust with neighbors through spontaneous personal

Although the commons were not well maintained by the new property management firm, traces of beauty remained, like this bed of spring flowers.

Teachers at the Sherman Community Center preschool brought the children to the commons frequently for picnics and other special events.

interactions, and they could experiment with environmental design without violating the autonomy of the community.

The basement was in terrible shape, but neighborhood young people in a Rutgers University 4-H summer training-and-employment program worked hard to clean, repair, and paint the space. At the end of summer the Resident Council and neighbors hosted a party for the young volunteers, who had worked so hard to clean and renovate the space. Everyone enjoyed the sumptuous feast, music, and dancing.

In the fall my students designed and built display panels, installed attractive lighting and furnishings, assembled cable-reel tables, and painted floors, trim, and pipes with cheerful colors. Our new workshop became a welcoming place with spaces for meetings, architectural studios, crafts, storage of salvaged materials, and demonstration areas open to the public. We named it Common Ground, inspired by the Common Ground of the Arts workshop space established and maintained during the mid-1960s in Detroit by visionary City Planning Director Charles Blessing. I arranged for resource people to conduct training sessions at Common Ground, including agricultural extension people from Rutgers University and Newark's Community Gardening Program who helped residents grow vegetables in the common areas around their buildings and in city-owned vacant lots. The Trust for Public Land provided training and also donated salvaged lumber for building a play structure. The center became an indoor commons, an incubator for creative expression, like the CUE workshop center in Columbus, Ohio. We celebrated the completion of construction at a gala Christmas party in 1979.

A fence surrounded the central commons and most of the smaller ones. I invited neighborhood organizations and residents to use and manage the commons and distributed keys to them. My faculty colleagues at the School of Architecture were surprised that I didn't object to the fence as they knew me as an advocate of free access to open spaces, so I invited them to meet with the residents who told

Residents used a large section of the central commons for growing vegetables and flowers.

them to leave their white liberalism at home. "If you live in the jungle where drugs and prostitution dominate, you need to protect any constructive improvement. Once we are less despairing, we can take the fence down." Their point was underscored after we laid the sod in the commons at 86 Brunswick, but before we installed the fence. A neighbor saw a third of the sod being hauled away on a pick-up truck. She caught the driver right before he turned the corner.

Daisy Hargraves, a dynamic community leader, ran the Sherman Community Center, which she had started twelve years earlier in her living room. The Center, in the same block as the central commons on Murray and Brunswick, had a daycare program that used the commons for many of its activities. Children planted vegetables and flowers, had picnics, and looked for Easter eggs. A gospel ensemble gave concerts in the commons. Mrs. Thomas, who ran a music school in her home on the other side of the commons, conducted graduation exercises in the commons, moving in a piano and inviting all her students and family members.

Long-time neighborhood resident Charles Mullin enjoyed decorating an evergreen tree in the central commons at Christmas time.

Neighborhood women prepared a sumptuous potluck feast to celebrate the opening of the Common Ground workshop center.

The Pueblo City Resident Council and neighbors expressed their appreciation for the young volunteers from the 4-H Summer Program, who had worked so hard to clean and renovate the Common Ground space, by throwing a street party with food, music, and dancing.

We created our Common Ground workshop commons in the basement of St. Luke AME Church across Murray Street from the central commons. Both the church and the workshop were destroyed by fire in the 1980s.

Neighbors cared for the gardens in the commons, planting flowers each year.

My students developed an exciting proposal for a Creation and Recreation Center on seven city-owned lots across the street as a memorial for Daisy Hargraves's son Lamont, who had been killed the year before. Five dilapidated and abandoned garages, being used for illicit activities, would be converted into studios and stores for local artists and craftspeople. Behind them would be an outdoor commons. A large cinderblock building would provide construction workshop space during the cold and wet winter months. Although the students overcame many hurdles, the project was never completed.

The day following one of my return visits to Common Ground in the 1980s, during the same hour of my visit the previous day, the boiler in St. Luke's basement exploded. The ensuing fire gutted the church and destroyed the workshop and all its stored equipment. Apparently the church did not have sufficient funding to properly maintain its equipment.

Revisiting Newark in the 1990s, I was shocked and saddened to discover that the central commons of Pueblo City had been bulldozed, eras-

Rather than construct a permanent barbecue pit, we installed a heavy flagstone surface onto which portable barbecues could be wheeled for special occasions and then removed to leave free space for other uses.

Mrs. Thomas's music school held recitals in the commons.

The commons at Murray and Brunswick, which had served the larger community, was bulldozed in the 1990s by the new property management firm.

ing everything, including the large trees. I learned that Sanford Gallanter had sold the management of his properties to a less caring owner. A new housing development had been built on the street, and the commons would have served those residents well. Nevertheless I know that those who participated in building and using the projects will remember it as an empowering experience.

Temporary Commons for Special Occasions

Animating Common Space with Flexible Stage Settings and Programs

When planning and staging conferences and gatherings in hotels, conference centers, and resort retreats, most people are unaware of and ignore the impact of the physical setting on the experience, thoughts, and behavior of their participants. Since making changes to architecture is perceived to be so cumbersome and expensive, people tend to suppress their awareness of how deeply they are affected, and often diminished, by the impersonal and regimented setting of most corporate, commercial, and institutional spaces.

The transformation of these spaces into animated, uplifting settings and green meeting places imbues users with a sense of well-being. Through participating in the instant transformation of spaces and the building of temporary commons, people begin to realize that they can become masters of their habitats and, by inference, of their lives.

Our physical surroundings must be responsive and flexible to accommodate our manifold and changing activities. This is similar to the flexibility that characterizes stage sets within which one can create subspaces. Tapping into a group's mission, one can create physical settings and programs that reflect and reinforce the aspiration and purpose of the meetings, fairs, or conferences.

I began creating commons as temporary stage settings for special events in the universities where I taught, to provide opportunities for my students of environmental design to have some hands-on experiences. They were able to build the temporary stage settings they designed and observe their use within the span of a semester. Since these temporary settings received intensive use during a short period of time, their effectiveness was immediately tested. In a sense these temporary stage settings became life-size simulation environments used for research on space-use. Later, as a consultant, I created temporary stage settings for conferences and other special events.

MARTIN LUTHER KING MEMORIAL

Sketch of the black flags that would create a setting for the memorial

Martin Luther King Jr. Memorial Commons

An Anti-racism and Social Justice Event

Massachusetts Institute of Technology (MIT), Boston, 1968

When I began to teach at the Massachusetts Institute of Technology (MIT) in 1968, I served as master's thesis advisor to three students, Steve Leff, Arthur Stern, and John Terry. These young men had started to design an innovative school as an abstract exercise, but their growing alarm about the Vietnam War had them considering how they might escape to Canada. Less and less able to continue work on their thesis, they came to me with their quandary. We discussed creating a memorial to the war dead in Vietnam.

Then, on Thursday, April 4, 1968, shortly after we began meeting, Dr. Martin Luther King Jr. was assassinated. I suggested to these students that we create a memorial event, which I hoped would elicit broad-based responses from students and faculty. Architectural history professor Henry Millon joined us in envisioning a physical environment that would enable students and faculty to express our sorrow, rage, guilt, remorse, frustration, and our hopes.

Word of our plan spread, and others joined

On Monday evening students gathered in the gymnasium to prepare the exhibit.

our small committee to work over the weekend. We started by sketching a rough design. We wanted to accommodate the overflow crowd from discussions in the auditorium and create a space for dialogue, including
• a "hall of issues" and "testimonial boards" where people could write their thoughts and respond to questions,
• tables and chairs for spontaneous group formation,
• a location for an open mike and places for booths.

The testimonial, or "feedback," boards were inspired by the work of my friend Phyllis Yampolsky, an artist and community activist who has developed many successful interactive installations.

Student paints a large portrait of Dr. King, sketched from a photo positive projected onto the canvas.

Student paints a quote onto a display board.

As we brainstormed how best to use the large space between Massachusetts Avenue and Kresge Hall, the students began building a model (at a half inch to a foot). The idea emerged to create a space for airing questions of racism and MIT's involvement as an institution. Central to our vision was an exhibit honoring the life of Martin Luther King with photographs and excerpts from his speeches. We kept our signs low near the street with the message

137

Early Tuesday morning students hung black streamers from the scaffolding and set up displays and booths.

Feedback or testimonial boards throughout the exhibit engaged visitors and gave them opportunities to express their thoughts and feelings.

"THE KING IS DEAD" and high near Kresge with a sign "LONG LIVE THE KING" mounted on scaffolding.

On Monday we presented the model to the Provost and the Dean of the School of Architecture, who gave us funds to buy construction materials and put us in touch with Physical Plant representatives and the Safety Officer. Physical Plant staff helped us acquire and transport lumber and scaffolding.

We formed committees, and some students made signs to recruit additional volunteers and solicit donations for supplies. Others posted the signs around the campus and spread the word within their departments. Other students contacted *The Boston Globe* and a local radio station to gather written and photographic material for the panels. A professor talked to his class about their apathy; his students left class to help with the exhibit.

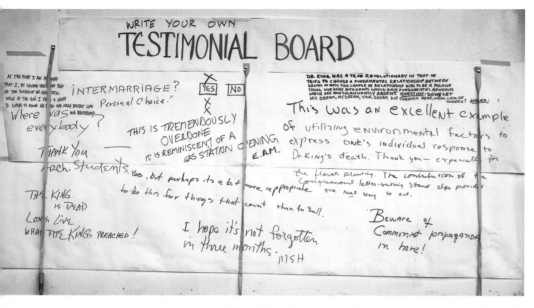

The widely divergent opinions expressed on the testimonial boards provided an opportunity for expanding awareness of racism and increased the potential for dialogue.

The concrete steps provided yet another opportunity for self-expression.

By Monday evening 250 volunteers from all departments gathered at the gymnasium ready to help. We divided into teams. To the sound of live music and hammers, we created display and testimonial boards and modular components for booths. Some people enlarged photographs for an outdoor exhibit on King's life and the civil rights struggle; the professor and technician in charge of the photo lab kept it open all night to finish the work. Other teams constructed and painted feedback boards, kiosks, and 4' x 8' freestanding exhibit panels. Others prepared the text for the display boards and did the lettering. One student sketched a huge portrait of King from a high-contrast projection positive, and many students cut black plastic ribbons into long streamers. The energy and teamwork amazed us all.

On Tuesday morning we constructed the mourning environment, attaching the black streamers to heavy string that was tied to scaffolding and stretched above the area. The streamers fluttered in the sad wintry wind. The photos were mounted, banners strung up, panels and booths, tables and chairs all in place. At around 8:30 AM representatives from a variety of student organizations began to arrive, occupying the booths where they distributed literature concerned with racism and engaged in dialogue with passers-by. The testimonial boards were quickly filled with people's statements, which generated a lot of discussion. One of the student-made signs questioned whether MIT should change its admission and curriculum policy so that many

Beginning at Massachusetts Avenue, the memorial continued uphill to Kresge Hall, the central building on the campus. Without impeding the flow of students and teachers entering and leaving the campus, the booths and exhibit materials offered opportunities for engagement and reflection.

Representatives of student organizations distributed relevant literature and engaged in dialogue with passers-by.

Things are not always as smooth as they appear on the surface. On Tuesday evening, physical plant staff, fearful that the flowers would freeze, dug up the geranium plants and kept them in a greenhouse overnight. Fortunately they replanted them early Wednesday morning.

more black students could attend, considering that there were only twenty-two American black graduates at the Institute in a total of 3,860.

Students also conducted panel discussions in the auditorium of Kresge Hall, challenging MIT to divest itself of military research and devote its resources to the struggle for civil rights. The auditorium did not fill up as anticipated, but the discussion also aired through speakers wired to the

outside. The open mike didn't catch on until the afternoon.

We had discussed the idea of a memorial planting of red geraniums when we met with the Physical Plant staff. Initially they opposed the idea but eventually agreed that we could use a part of the lawn they had not returfed. I bought 250 red geraniums and set them next to the freshly dug round bed, with trowels and a sign: "Please help

yourself and plant a red flower." As the day went by, people stopped to dig, and a brilliant patch of red flowers grew on the green lawn. Everyone who participated planted the flowers with great care. The appropriate redness and aliveness of the geraniums made the planting an unmistakable act of faith to accompany the anguished tribute to the slain leader. Participants and visitors were deeply moved, and

we succeeded in creating a very powerful memorial. Local newspapers reported on it extensively, and AP and UPI carried the story.

Visitors wrote a broad range of comments on the testimonial boards, among them:

> *This was an excellent example of utilizing environmental factors to express one's individual response to*

The heart of the memorial commons was in the plaza in front of Kresge Hall.

Dr. King's death. Thank you especially for the flower planting. The contribution of the Congressional letter-writing stand also provides one real way to act.

I hope it's not forgotten in three months.

Is this just a cheap catharsis?

Beware of Communist propaganda in here.

The exhibit remained up on Wednesday, and although most of the groups for the booths did not show up the second morning, by noon the tables and chairs were in use and the space felt alive again. Later in the afternoon the Caravan Theater performed amidst the banners and scaffolding. Afterward we met with the administration and Physical Plant staff to discuss the next steps. Eventually we all agreed that the exhibit had made its impact and should come down.

The students documented their process during those few days of intense activity and made that information available to others, eager to share their discovery that even within a rigid institutional environment it was possible to create a setting for airing timely issues and feelings. As a result, other colleges and groups displayed the exhibit.

The physical and meditative act of planting a flower offered a different level of engagement and was an effective counterpoint to the testimonial boards, booths, and sitting areas.

Student–Designed and Built Environments

My original interest in teaching at MIT had been sparked when I heard about the spontaneous self-help construction by architectural students to personalize their drafting rooms. The students scrounged materials and worked clandestinely to shift cinder block partitions and erect a series of mezzanines or platforms to make room for individual and small group study spaces. I contacted a faculty member who had been a volunteer for the Neighborhood Renewal Corps of Philadelphia, and he introduced me to other faculty. Much to my delight the school offered me a position.

Based on the successful staging of the King memorial and the impressive work that my three master's students had done to personalize their study

spaces, I suggested that they continue in this vein, and focus their thesis project on humanizing physical settings in the MIT environment. With broad participation of other students, they created a small sitting area next to a vending machine and transformed the long impersonal hallways into a communication environment that displayed the research of scientists at MIT. The heart of their thesis expressed the idea that when students (and faculty and staff) contribute to designing and building their campus environment, they feel more connected, more a part of the college community.

Later the personalizing of study spaces became a special attraction of MIT's School of Architecture. They even published a booklet, "How to Transform Impersonal Study Spaces," which included directions for safety precautions. These successful community design-and-build efforts led to the development of the Community Projects Laboratory, which continued to humanize the campus environment and rendered community design-and-build service to Boston's low-income communities.

The students designed and built this sociability setting around a vending machine.

Bulletin boards and displays encouraged communication and brightened and humanized otherwise impersonal hallways.

Engaging informational displays about MIT innovators inspired a sense of appreciation and pride in the campus community.

Children, Nature, and the Urban Environment

A Symposium-fair

George Washington University, Washington, D.C., May 1975

In 1974 I joined the planning team for a symposium-fair on Children, Nature, and the Urban Environment to be held at George Washington University in Washington, D.C. The primary sponsor was the Pinchot Institute of Environmental Forestry Research of the U.S. Forest Service, and we developed the event in cooperation with Cook College Department of Environmental Resources at Rutgers, the State University of New Jersey, and George Washington University's Department of Human Kinetics and Leisure Studies and School of Education. This symposium-fair brought together a diverse group of participants—educators, planners, psychologists, park rangers, artists, designers, college students, teenagers, and children.

Our goal was to explore "How the Natural Environment Affects Children's Growth in Cities"—sharing experiences, distilling ideas, and generating practical recommendations for fostering beneficial relationships between urban children and nature. After I expressed hopes that we could stage the gathering as an inspiring event, I was hired as symposium manager and charged with staging of ceremony and environment. I looked forward to

Children's art in the ground-floor windows of the Marvin Center created a lively, inspiring ambience for the symposium.

animating the gathering, to enriching it with verbal and visual presentations of art, music, movement, and beautifully presented healthy food.

Outreach materials included this poetic statement: "We all share dreams and hopes for children and for children yet to be and, caring, shall assemble to recall the child within. To gather for a symposium on tender human growth, in this alarming age of nature's destruction and nuclear peril is an act of faith. Joined in common fate let us together affirm and nurture life on earth."

The image on our posters and letterhead depicted six kids on a homemade river raft, like Mark Twain's Huckleberry Finn, pushing along the waters of the East River with the Manhattan skyline in the distance. Water is such a powerful image of

strength and vitality, even stronger than trees or vegetation. The image had been generated for the "Sketchbook of Ideas" that I developed at Long Island University in 1965.

I engaged six friends to work with me and decorate the large impersonal C. H. Marvin Student Union Building with banners, plants, and silhouettes, and to transform it into a warm and friendly space with sociability settings throughout.

We hung 170 colorful banners symbolizing the elements of the environment. The well-known children's book illustrator Norman Laliberté and his students at Newton College in Massachusetts had made them for the 50th anniversary conference of the American Institute of Planners in 1967. At the end of our symposium, we held a raffle and

Colorful banners helped to humanize the drab institutional environment.

One hundred seventy banners created by children's book illustrator Norman Laliberté and his students were hung throughout the symposium space.

sold the banners as a fundraiser for the nonprofit who had made them available to us.

Drawing on connections I had made in 1963 while coordinating the Landscape Technician Training Program, a federally funded program for high school dropouts, I borrowed large colorful plants from the U.S. Botanic Gardens. We used large freestanding cardboard tubes about four feet high to elevate and support the plants and bring them to eye level. We then moved them around as needed to frame various spaces.

In the lobbies and on the third floor terrace we installed exhibits prepared by organizations such as the Youth Conservation Corps, Job Corps, YMCA, and Washington Youth Gardens. The American Horticultural Society mounted an exhibit on their "People-Plant Interaction Program. The director of the

Plants from the U.S. Botanic Gardens rested on large freestanding cardboard tubes to bring them to eye level.

One of the plenary panel discussions on the first day of the symposium

Feedback and message boards increased participation and helped to democratize the event.

Beautification and Ecology Program for the D.C. public schools coordinated displays of children's art from local elementary schools under the theme "Our Environment." Participants also brought exhibits, and others were created during the event.

We invited participants to come early and take part in environmental arts workshops, such as "Green Fun" by artist-photographer Maryanne Gjersvik, a continuous workshop making toys, games, and rhythms from natural materials taken from children's folklore, and "A Time to Play" by Elaine Ostroff, which provided opportunities for personal play though improvisations with movement, sound, and space. We also encouraged par-

ticipants to bring photographs to display on special exhibit structures, or slides or film to show in the Marvin Center Theater. We equipped all meeting rooms with extensive feedback boards, and set aside rooms for spontaneous group discussions.

After registration on Monday afternoon participants enjoyed a sumptuous Welcome Dinner with official greetings from the sponsoring organizations, an opening talk by Mary Conway Kohler, Director of the National Commission on Resources for Youth, and a poetry reading titled "The Weeds Asserting Themselves" in which poets and children viewed the natural environment.

On Tuesday morning and afternoon, panel

Storytellers and musicians engaged the attention of children and adults.

Artists worked with the children to make beautiful wall hangings by weaving together colorful thread, yarn, and ribbons.

discussions focused on the value of natural settings for psychological well-being, human development, and creativity. Panelists included anthropologist Margaret Mead, humanistic geographer Yi Fu Tuan, psychoanalyst Harold Searles, environmental design researcher Mayer Spivack, and geographer and environmental psychologist Roger Hart. Roger brought along eighteen children from Vermont with whom he was conducting an eighteen-month research proj-

ect. He had formed such a deeply trusting relationship with these children that they had shared with him secret hiding places no other adult had seen. Now they would have the opportunity to interact with inner-city children.

Before the conference we constructed temporary children's play areas and organized storytelling and crafts. We engaged artists to lead activities and solicited donations of salvaged materials from

151

New games shift the focus away from winning and toward the fun of playing.

the university, a local art supply company, an ad agency, the Boston Children's Museum, the International Paper Company, and National Tire Wholesale. Mark Francis and Ray Lorenzo from Harvard University Graduate School of Design developed the Children's Resource and Discovery Room, which served as a center for children visiting and participating in the conference. It housed interactive exhibits and provided a focal point for scheduled workshops with various local elementary school classes.

At midday Tuesday participants explored

"Early Childhood Playscapes from Memory" and engaged in small discussion groups. The evening was devoted to film presentations and discussions.

On Wednesday and Thursday we arranged to accommodate the broad range of interest by scheduling a multitude of parallel seminars and workshops. We encouraged brief presentations that would stimulate discussion about the value of nature experiences for city children. Four parallel discussion tracks were available—Theory and Research on Children and the Natural Environment, Education, Community Approaches to Environmental Quality, and Design and Planning of Children's Environments.

On Wednesday I scheduled a lunchtime outing to the intimate and serene campus of Mt. Vernon College. I arranged for representatives of the New Games Foundation in San Francisco, who were developing cooperative games that transcend

While waiting in line for a buffet lunch participants socialized and enjoyed the natural setting.

Cooperative games gave everyone a sense of community and a hearty appetite.

The small round tables, including some cable reels, encouraged conversation and community. Small centerpieces added a ceremonial feel to mealtimes.

An outdoor area we covered with a large colorful parachute canopy for shaded gatherings

cultural, racial, social, and economic barriers, to engage participants in activities on the large lawns. Afterward we enjoyed a beautiful Middle Eastern buffet.

Colorful displays of healthy food at each meal pleased the tastes of the diverse participants, and I hired musicians to provide soothing background music during the meals. When I first learned that a large food vending company would supply the meals, I was apprehensive, but fortunately I knew the owner of the company because we both sat on

The children loved the tires and tubes we provided, which offered plenty of opportunities for playful improvisation.

Covering each other with a stack of inner tubes was endlessly entertaining.

Stretching exercises afforded a welcome relief from hours of sitting during presentations and discussions.

Improvisations with movement, sound, and space provided fun and relaxation and helped participants get in touch with the child within.

the board of the Washington Center of Metropolitan Studies. I contacted him and made a proposal: "We have an ecologically oriented audience," I explained. "Why not experiment with healthy food?" I convinced him that in addition to traditional dishes we should have organic food, beautifully displayed.

I worked with a dietician for nine months to plan all the meals, which we served buffet style in the pleasant and spacious dining facilities of the Marvin Center. Tables seated no more than eight to ten, and simple centerpieces and candles adorned each one to enhance the festive atmosphere. We made nourishing

The potted plants that had brightened the tables became keepsakes for the departing children.

snacks available in the meeting lounges, and we published a detailed menu, which included inspiring quotes from the Tassajara Cookbook and the Tassajara Bread Book, along with background information on the food we served. Curious about a dish called Muscoe Vegetable Soup, on the last day's lunch menu, I had a good laugh when I learned that it referred to leftover produce—the "must go" vegetables.

For those who needed a break from sitting in workshops, we offered relaxation exercises. I engaged a friend to come down from Boston to conduct yoga-like exercises, which helped participants relax after sitting for too long in lecture chairs.

Upon parting we presented each of the children, those from Vermont and the local children from D.C., with a small colorful potted plant to take home and nurture. Smiles and waves mixed with tears as the Vermont children boarded the buses that would carry them home.

Overview of the central convention area. Jose Rivera, whose organization, United Tremont Trades, constructed the wooden buildings in the foreground, characterized the larger one as a "South Bronx model home—two stories with lots of windows, a balcony, and a patio for raising a few chickens."

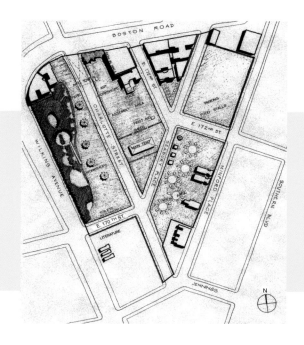

The People's Convention

An Urban Outdoor Gathering to Build a New Political Party Devoted to Social Justice

South Bronx, NY, 1980

During the summer of 1980, I volunteered, along with the other environmental designers I recruited, to help create a campsite and gathering space that would accommodate 1,000 delegates to the "People's Convention" and 2,000 guests. The site was the infamous Charlotte Street in New York's South Bronx, a ten-block-square wasteland of rubble that had once been apartment buildings.

Between 1968 and 1980 ten thousand buildings were burned by arson-for-profit rings in response to "redlining" by banks, who refused to make property-improvement loans in so-called blighted areas. Two hundred thousand people were displaced from their neighborhoods. Businesses fled. The phrase "Broken

Promises" was stenciled high up on buildings and visible from far away. Presidents Carter and Reagan, as well as local politicians, had visited the area and declared their commitment to repair the devastation but had done nothing as conditions worsened. Clusters of vacant high-rise buildings stood ominously in and around the fields of rubble, pocked with endless rows of broken windows.

During the previous year a broad-ranging coalition of grassroots organizations had been meeting with the goal of developing a united front. They were frustrated and disillusioned by the Democratic Party's empty promises and failure to address the problem of unemployment, inadequate housing,

The landscape on which the campsite and convention assembly would be constructed was piled high with rubble. We needed earth-moving equipment to clear space.

Volunteers burned paper trash and gathered bricks, tires, and wood for reuse.

GEORGE COHEN

160

Volunteer architects discuss the plans.

Karl orchestrates the volunteer effort of barnraising the People's Convention site.

and decaying infrastructure. Self-identified as the "Coalition for a People's Alternative in 1980," these community organizers envisioned a gathering that would precede the Democratic National Convention, due to begin on Monday, August 11, in Madison Square Garden. This alternate "People's Convention" would serve simultaneously as a protest and an organizing event.

The overarching goal of the organizers was to reconcile the conflicting philosophies, strategies, and goals within the people's movement and form a third national political party. As designers we envisioned an environment that would facilitate dialogue among the many divergent groups, deepening their understanding of one another's problems and perspectives and helping them move toward consensus. We also wanted to create a model for urban community living with child care, adventure playgrounds, and green markets. We imagined easy-to-assemble geodesic domes for temporary shelter, explored the use of solar energy, and thought about how to use the vast quantities of brick debris from the demolition of buildings.

Activists and organizers eagerly share their vision and encourage the volunteers. Puerto Rican flag in the background.

161

Supporters gather to share food and socialize after working hard to clear the site.

Construction got underway in June with half a day of donated bulldozer time. In addition to clearing rubble we needed to grade the sloping terrain into a few level terraces. One would accommodate a huge tent for the assembly of delegates and others would house task-force gatherings and temporary quarters and amenities for the attendees. We decided to push the perimeters of spaces where activities and gatherings would take place. Several taller piles served as landmarks. Volunteers from the various groups in the coalition worked every weekend alongside neighborhood residents to clear and prepare the site.

Coalition organizers held a press conference to publicize the "People's Convention and Festival" with the goal of attracting supporters and endorsers

and recruiting volunteers to help prepare the site. A well-publicized work party and picnic on the Fourth of July attracted many new volunteers, who worked with their bare hands and with loaned and donated wheelbarrows, rakes, picks, and shovels to gather and sort reusable materials and prepare the ground for construction. The huge pile of metal debris we had gathered by the end of the day dramatized the reality of this ghostlike environment of disintegration, disaffection, and resurgence.

A key organizer and spokesman for the event, José Rivera, was founding director of United Tremont Trades (UTT), an organization of several hundred Latino and black construction workers dedicated to finding and fighting for jobs. His work for the People's Convention launched Rivera into

Volunteers construct the broad steps that joined the different levels of the site.

Musical rhythms made the work more enjoyable.

GEORGE COHEN

a lifetime career in the New York City Council and State Assembly. UTT members and other volunteers contributed their skills to creating infrastructure—bringing electricity and hot and cold running water to the site and constructing three wooden buildings using scrounged and donated materials, including a central building, affectionately called "The White House." Their efficiency and speed demonstrated how much the community could do with minimal resources in contrast with the government's apparent inability to do anything to create housing.

Every weekend leading up to the event volunteers and residents combed the rubble-strewn land, carefully stockpiling salvageable materials. They fashioned sets of broad steps from salvaged beams, filled in with bricks, to connect the terraces that had been leveled by the bulldozer. Working together physically to build the campsite nurtured solidarity among the diverse members of the coalition, which was composed of Latino, black, American Indian, gay-lesbian, feminist, socialist, religious, antiwar, anti-nuclear, and tenant rights groups. Months of collaborative planning and preparation made the participants more receptive to dialogue and did a lot to facilitate agreement on the unity statement at the end of the gathering.

We did not find a source for materials to construct geodesic domes; instead we put up parachutes to protect workshops and caucuses from the sun.

The organizers recruited artists to create posters and flyers; banners, murals, and signs; sculptures; and a welcoming gateway structure. Architects and

163

The central pole supporting the parachute was used for posting notes and information about the proceedings.

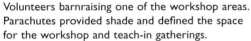

Volunteers barnraising one of the workshop areas. Parachutes provided shade and defined the space for the workshop and teach-in gatherings.

Participants improvised, moving their chairs to whatever configuration would be most effective and most comfortable.

landscape architects like myself were asked to design and prepare a site plan of tents, kiosks, and signage; an adventure playground for children attending with their parents; and a "park" area with seating.

The layout of the campsite made it possible for the convention to conduct its assemblies, teach-ins, cultural activities, and social life in the most efficient way. In addition to the assembly tent and the parachutes, UTT members, artists, and other volunteers designed and constructed kiosks, display boards, clotheslines for posting materials being

Passers-by were invited to contribute a hand print to a giant "Unity" mural that was created in large panels that were assembled and mounted on a nearby wall.

Artists Elizabeth Clark and Valentine Goroshko designed this "information structure," which they called "Reconstruction Project," to display information and to symbolize grassroots reconstruction of society.

We created spaces for convention participants to gather in a peaceful natural setting by thinning existing stands of volunteer trees.

Plan for Coalition Park and the adjacent workshop areas. The dark areas are tree covered; the light patches are clearings made by thinning the trees. The main assembly area was on the other side of Charlotte Street.

generated, and platforms and soapboxes to encourage the free expression of ideas.

We created an instant park, which we named Coalition Park, by thinning self-seeded stands of ailanthus, poplar, and sycamore trees in an adjacent former creekbed. The clearings became spaces where people could gather, surrounded by nature, to dialogue and socialize.

View from the park: the workshop areas were shaded from the sun by parachutes.

Overview of the instant Coalition Park and several gathering places for workshops and small groups

GEORGE COHEN

On Friday morning, August 8, South Bronx community leaders and convention organizers welcomed the delegates. The opening plenary session was devoted to five-minute presentations by delegates on "Why We Are Here." Small local food vendors took advantage of the opportunity to feed the delegates and guests. Volunteers from several dozen organizations set up booths with literature and buttons. Participants had free time in the middle of the day to explore, socialize, and network. Interactive art projects resulted in murals that were hung on surrounding buildings. In the afternoon participants could choose among workshop sessions devoted to particular constituencies and issues. The organizers

circulated drafts of a proposed unity statement to be finalized on Sunday and presented to Democratic Convention delegates. The evening was set aside for musical and theatrical performances. UTT volunteers constructed a fence with salvaged wood and chicken wire to protect the sound equipment.

Saturday, August 9, began with a panel discussion on "The Economic Crisis and the Quality of Life," followed by discussions in small groups. Activists and leaders of grassroots organizations convened task forces on particular topics–government repression and prisons, independent political action, labor, racism, sexism, lesbian/gay rights, energy and anti-nuclear, international/militarism, land and

First aid area

167

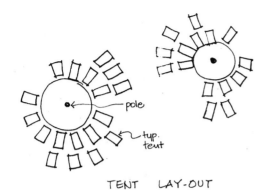

TENT LAY-OUT

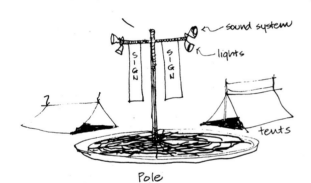

sound system
lights
SIGN
SIGN
tents

Pole

SLOGANS
SIGNS

Delegates brought their own tents. We designed an arrangement in which each group would pitch their tents around a central pole, with a crossbar to support lights and speakers and display identifying signage.

Convention participants gathered in the assembly tent.

In our temporary adventure playground children used bricks and lumber that volunteers had stockpiled from the rubble to build structures of their own.

View of the assembly tent from an adjacent gutted building

GEORGE COHEN

rural development, and tenants and neighborhood organizing.

In the afternoon, a panel on "War, Militarism, and Liberation Struggles" was followed by a stretch break and a panel on "Struggles for Democratic Rights." The task forces gathered to make plans for the future and to discuss a new draft of the unity statement and forge agreement prior to the next morning's plenary session.

Saturday night was a rich cultural event with multi-ethnic singers, musicians, and theater groups.

On Sunday morning, August 10, delegates gathered in small groups to discuss the unity statement and to prepare for a march and demonstration in Madison Square Garden that afternoon across from the Democratic Convention. The organizers wanted to condemn the empty promises and lies of the two political parties and to demand that the voice of the people be heard. "The Declaration of Charlotte Street," later published as a four-page tabloid in English and Spanish, outlined a people's agenda for jobs, a decent standard of living, and a safe environment within the context of equality, freedom, democracy, peace, and a just international order.

Literature
tables

Marching through Times Square
to Madison Square Garden

The march ended with a demonstration in
front of Madison Square Garden where the
Democratic Convention was being held.

Police estimated 5,000 participants in the
march from Columbus Circle to Madison Square
Garden and 10,000 at the rally. Participants in
demonstrations at several locations converged at
Madison Square Garden for the rally. The Day of
Protest, another movement forming in Central Park
planned to disrupt the Democratic Convention proceedings, but the People's Convention organizers
decided not to endorse that strategy.

The organizers invited some participants to
stay on until August 14 to work on the site in the
hope of leaving something of value there for the
people of the South Bronx. We hoped that the
campsite would evolve into a community-wide
commons, a social and recreational hub of the surrounding area.

From Restoration to Gentrification

Much to our surprise, the City took advantage of the cleared, leveled terraces by planting them with wildflowers. This was a pilot demonstration project for greening large tracts of land made vacant by urban renewal demolition projects. After scattering topsoil, motorized vehicles hydroseeded the land. Months later acres of colorful wildflower meadows transformed the area, lifting the spirits of local residents. This cover crop of wildflowers could have, over years, produced fertile soil for urban agriculture, but the city's purpose was primarily to attract developers.

When I visited the site later, in the mid-1980s, the first two models of suburban, ranch-style homes had been built. Much later I learned that all the South Bronx wildflower meadows were replaced with ranch-style housing. This real-estate development was driven by profit rather than by considerations of social equity and sustainability. It did little or nothing to serve community needs since the new homes were not affordable for the displaced residents of demolished apartment buildings. The existing infrastructure that could have supported high-density housing was wasted, and the new construction resulted in pockets of gentrification amidst decades-old decay and disrepair.

The rubble-filled lots were hydroseeded after the event and transformed into wildflower meadows.

Suburban ranch-style homes later replaced the wildflower meadows.

171

During lunchtime people gathered to share food and conversation amidst the sparkling fountain, lush green foliage, and blossoming flowers.

Healthy Cities Commons

Sharing Grassroots Projects That Improve People's Quality of Life

San Francisco Hilton Hotel, December 8–11, 1993

Leonard Duhl, a psychiatrist who teaches public health and urban planning at the University of California at Berkeley, helped spearhead the Healthy Cities movement. Its programs, sponsored by the United Nations World Health Organization, have initiated partnerships between citizens and government and have inspired cooperation among the most diverse endeavors and people. I met Len in the early 1960s when he lectured at the University of Pennsylvania where I was teaching. Later we collaborated on a survey for the establishment of a national service corps. When I moved to the San Francisco Bay Area, I reconnected with him and was delighted when he invited me to partici-

pate in planning and staging the First International Healthy Cities and Communities Conference.

The conference, at the San Francisco Hilton Hotel, would bring together 1,700 participants, including 450 presenters from all over the world, to share projects generated in 1,000 cities and communities. After six months of brainstorming and deliberations the conference structure took shape and the Planning Committee endorsed the creation of a commons. We decided to sandwich it between the commercial exhibit area in the rear of the Great Ballroom and the rows of 2,000 chairs that faced the main stage.

The commons would provide a place for

Volunteers meet in Karl and Nicole's living room to plan and design the commons.

participants to meet face-to-face, share issues and concerns, and tell their stories in a personal way. I was delighted by the opportunity to demonstrate the transformation and humanizing of the existing institutional hotel ballroom setting.

Barnraising the Commons with Volunteers

In a spirit of cooperation and dedication consistent with the strategies of Healthy Cities, we recruited 110 volunteers to help create the commons in exchange for free admission to the conference. Some were to function as hosts to make people feel comfortable, especially those who came from far afield with potential language barriers. We also needed volunteers to construct our display panels; scout for, procure and assemble building, plant,

and exhibit material; install the commons; mount the Healthy Cities Projects Gallery; look after the interactive exhibits; and document the process in writing, video, and photographs. We would invest tremendous energy and creativity in the creation of the commons, and we wanted to capture its fleeting moment of existence for others.

We allocated two-thirds of our limited $20,000 budget to hiring a part-time Volunteer Coordinator and a part-time Outreach Coordinator. I asked for a small stipend to design, construct, and produce the commons, but most of my work was as a volunteer. Prioritizing spending on personnel over materials was consistent with Healthy Cities' people-intensive rather than capital-intensive strategies. Some of our highly qualified volunteers assumed responsibil-

Installing the free-standing panels that defined the circumference of the commons

ity for coordinating construction, documentation, and live musical entertainment. The considerable discounts and donations that we received in building material, plant material, and film also made it possible for us to stay within our budget. Given a conference like this, with an approximate cash flow of $500,000 and in-kind donations of $300,000, a budget of $50,000 for a commons of this scope would have been more appropriate.

We worked in close collaboration and liaison with conference coordinator Judy Mings, her staff, and the Hilton Hotel. Suzanne Karasik, whom we engaged as Volunteer Coordinator, worked tirelessly orchestrating the energies of the volunteers—recruiting, training, and coordinating work schedules so that volunteers could attend the workshops of their

choosing. Volunteers included architects, landscape architects, artists, musicians, writers, scientists, social workers, students, and many others. Bi-monthly potluck gatherings swelled in ranks each time we met.

During August and September we submitted designs and estimates, proposing to carve out an area of 100 by 50 feet in the Great Ballroom of the hotel. We would define the space by surrounding the commons with a freestanding exhibit structure. The exhibits would reinforce the information shared in the plenary sessions and workshops with images of Healthy Cities' projects and other innovative community-empowering efforts mounted and displayed on both sides of the structure. Two- and three-dimensional exhibits, employing a broad range of artistic expression, would dramatize our

Jo Hanson and her volunteers collected and attached redwood branches to the display panels of the exhibit structure above the "tree trunks" she had constructed with cardboard.

The Redwood Arbor was one of five entrances to the commons.

concerns for ecological sustainability and social justice.

We researched healthy building materials and constructed panels of three-ply cardboard in reinforced wooden frames. We joined the forty-five lightweight but rigid panels with metal electrical conduit pipes. Some of the details we necessarily worked out during construction.

Café de la Paz in Berkeley generously provided a staging ground for assembling the display panels and storing exhibit material. To help us stay within our budget, volunteer contractors made building materials and hardware available to us at wholesale prices. After a hard day collaboratively constructing

our commons display wall, one of our volunteer architects, Mark Gorrell, aptly remarked,

What I most enjoy doing, like today, is working with people voluntarily, with no boss, with no domineering authority, everyone contributing their own ideas. The good feeling that evolved among us also made it possible for us to solve a lot of problems that came up.

Volunteers also shepherded numerous participatory activities that took place in the commons, which served as a kind of "Green Room," the room backstage in the theater where actors can meet. A

Children's toys imaginatively fashioned from tin cans hung from the trellised top of the Arbor of Creative Recycling.

Each cart in the Healthy Food Arbor contained a bounty of borrowed fresh produce we would return to stores. Suspended garden gloves decorated the arbor trellis.

growing sense of community developed among the volunteers and extended to conference participants. The dedication of the volunteers far exceeded their work commitment of so many hours before or during the conference. A common vision of a transformed society and an opportunity to contribute individually and communally to its realization provided fertile ground for our collaborative effort.

Installing the Commons

We had two days before the opening of the conference to install the exhibit. On our first day, when we needed to be at the hotel loading dock at 8 a.m., our caravan crossed the Bay Bridge to San Francisco just as the rising sun illuminated the city and surrounding water with shimmering golden light. We shared a warm breakfast at a truck-stop café, which charged us for the long day of work ahead. At the hotel, volunteers unloaded each truck and station wagon and took the material upstairs on dollies. We then raised the display wall, lifting sections and joining them to define the circumference of the commons. A zig-zag placement created spatial niches within which intimate meetings could take place. Volunteers placed our fountain, display material, trees, and flowers. At the last minute we learned that fewer exhibitors than expected had signed up, so we used the extra space to create a Commons

Junior high school students painted banner images for display.

Connie, a senior from St. Mary's Center, came to the Commons to see her art work—a life-sized body collage she made in collaboration with a ten-year-old volunteer from St. Patrick's Church. Connie talked at length about how important it is for older people to be connected with young ones.

CIIS students proudly showed one of the two murals they created for the commons, depicting their visions of a healthy city.

Annex. We also eliminated the rear wall of the Commons Stage so that users of the annex could see and hear the musicians.

The "Welcoming Arbor" Installations

We installed a "Welcome to the Commons" banner at the main entrance and 8-by-8 foot entrance arbors at the four corners that provided spaces for creative installations by local artists.

• Berkeley sculptor Susan Leibovitz Steinman framed the Healthy Food Arbor with eighteen shopping carts in three tiers, which functioned as display cases for the essentials for healthy urban food and food sources. She explained her intent to reclaim the image of the shopping cart, originally a symbol of progress and economic well-being, which has become associated with unhealthy over-processed and over-packaged food, ecological abuses, and homelessness. The Merritt College Horticultural Program suspended gardening gloves and displayed flats of seedlings to represent the importance of growing healthy fresh produce close to home.

Colorful community art exhibits covered the walls that framed the commons.

• San Francisco artist Jo Hanson created the Redwood Arbor, inspired by the idea of redwoods as the wise elders of the natural world.

• San Francisco's Eye Gallery developed the Arbor of First Exposure, a photo installation called "Youth Opportunities through Photography," which presented the work of Bay Area youths-at-risk.

• The Sanitary Landfill Company produced the Arbor of Creative Recycling, which depicted a visual history of recycling in San Francisco, from the horse and wagon days to current programs.

The Healthy Cities Projects Gallery

We contacted Healthy Cities coordinators worldwide to request project material to mount on 2-by-2-foot display panels. We also asked fifty community-based projects in the San Francisco Bay Area to provide displays, and arranged site tours with them for our conference participants. In addition, we invited exhibits from art teachers at local community centers, elementary and high schools, and colleges, as well as prominent artists whose work is consistent with the vision and goals of the Healthy Cities movement. We received abundant material, especially from community centers that conducted art programs.

Among the student exhibits, the work from Calvin Simmons Junior High School in Oakland stood out. They mounted large, colorful mandalas and smaller banners above the exhibits in the commons.

The Eco-Action Team, a group of anthropology students from the California Institute of Integral Studies, created two colorful murals. They first generated long lists of images reflective of healthy cities during three envisioning sessions—each lasting for several hours. The campus was then invited to three four-hour sessions to paint the murals using ideas from the feedback board.

Greening the Commons

Our all-out effort to create a healthy and uplifting environment began by replacing all the artificial plants in the ballroom with live greenery. We visited greenhouses and nurseries to request donated plants

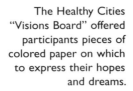

An Issues Feedback Board gave participants a chance to express their concerns, observations, and suggestions.

The Healthy Cities "Visions Board" offered participants pieces of colored paper on which to express their hopes and dreams.

Adjacent tables, chairs, and pens and paper facilitated the process of writing vision statements.

in exchange for publicity. What could not be donated, we rented at discounted prices. We framed the commons with ten 10-to-12-foot tall Ficus benjamina. The canopy of foliage towered above the exhibit structures and three large trees greened the stage. To them we attached tags with research information from the National Aeronautics and Space Administration that explained how live plants improve the quality of the air we breathe.

Three-Dimensional Exhibits

Shane Eagleton exhibited his ecological woodcarving, "Walk Lightly on the Earth," made of salvaged lumber engraved with intricate patterns of endangered animals, plants, and people.

"Bench Art" was painted by John Armstrong, a formerly homeless senior citizen at St. Mary's Center in Oakland. Artist Roxanne Hill's "No Place to Stay" art project there gave homeless senior citizens an opportunity to portray their problems and needs through drawing and painting. Influenced by public exhibitions of this work, Oakland's Department of Aging moved to provide shelter for homeless seniors.

Pedal Express and its cargo of herbs, flowers, and fresh produce attracted a lot of attention.

During the first night reception in the commons, a special festively decorated buffet table overflowed with food.

Master woodworker Scott Constable used salvaged lumber to build a simple elegant bench on which we mounted the art, and three stools we used to display exhibit literature.

Arrowsmith Academy high school student Jessica De Jonghe exhibited two life-size paper maché figurines of assertive women.

Elise Gay from the National Center for Appropriate Technology wheeled a unique tricycle into the hotel, decorated with a canopy sheltering a large container filled with herbs, flowers, and fresh produce. Pedal Express, a new cooperative bicycle delivery service, supported her credo that the commerce of a city is enhanced by sustainable, non-polluting transport.

To humanize the questionable elegance of the hotel decor, another well-known local artist Slobodan Dan Paitch introduced a note of humor when he suspended an undulating brightly colored serpent from the ceiling and hung hula hoops, which hovered whimsically over the commons.

Participatory Activities

The commons became the hub of activities at the conference, its convivial atmosphere supporting relaxation, communication, and creativity. A model Healthy Cities space, it functioned as a catalyst for ideas and action and enabled participants to share

Len Duhl, who spearheaded the conference, studies an envisioning chart created by participants.

their inspired visions and work. Interactive exhibits and activities nurtured a growing sense of community among the participants. Healthy Cities activists contributed to the Signing-in Gallery, which gave them an opportunity to attach their cards to the board and to describe their projects in digest form, with their names and contact information. The cards facilitated networking and provided source material for a Healthy Cities directory.

At the World Map and Eco-Regions of the Continents panel, they had an opportunity to locate and mark their projects with pins. This showed vividly the worldwide span of Healthy Cities projects and placing cities in bioregional context.

Something called a Healthy Cities "-Visions Board" was set up to provide a place where people could express their hopes and dreams using paper and pens available on nearby tables. The words and sketches generated were placed on this feedback board that offered guidance and imagery for other participants and community muralists.

The Visions Board was a variation of the "American Town Hall at America's Reunion on the Mall," created by Phyllis Yampolsky for President Clinton's first inauguration festival. (The sole interactive event at the Clinton inauguration, that giant "wall," now at the Clinton Library, amassed 12,000 messages in two days.)

Oakland artist Leah Korican conducted a Wish Cloth Workshop and invited participants to paint their hopes and wishes for healthy cities on colorful fabrics of about a foot square. Participants covered many display panels with their wish cloths, further animating the commons.

Performers played soothing live music on the Commons Stage during lunchtime.

This double exposure captures the exuberance of participants dancing to "Passionate Grace," a band from Oakland.

Some participants also made their own Wood Rubbings with artist Shane Eagleton. Visitors made rubbings with crayons on paper and took them home as cherished possessions.

The hotel set up a festive food counter offering salads and sandwiches. Although we had been unable to persuade the hotel's catering service to prepare a special Healthy Foods menu, people flocked to the commons anyway, drawn by the ambience and opportunity for socializing.

My wife Nicole Milner, a pianist-composer, performed and coordinated the musical offerings. The musicians included Philip Rosheger, a classical guitarist who had studied with Andres Segovia; Lisa Moskow, who had trained on the sarod with master Ali Akbar Khan; and Edie Hartshorne, schooled in Western and Japanese classical music, on the koto and flute. The music filled the commons space with enchanting rhythms that contributed to an atmosphere of receptivity and sharing.

On the morning of the opening I felt pangs of doubt. What if people who came from other parts of the world preferred to explore the beautiful city of San Francisco rather than frequent the commons? What if they tired of waiting in long

Around the tables in the commons people shared stories, ideas, and visions, forging new friendships and alliances and expanding old ones.

queues at the hotel's buffet table at lunch time and decided instead to visit some of the wonderful restaurants in the area? I felt a heavy burden of responsibility toward our volunteers and others whom we had inspired with our expectations—which I knew many people considered unrealistic. I was relieved when the commons exceeded my wildest expectations, both in its colorful and exuberant appearance and as a dynamic hub of activities.

Visitors said that being in the commons made them happy to be alive, that it strengthened them and reinforced them in their purpose. Afterward one attendee described the commons as "thought-provoking as any city or community center could be." Many conference participants said they never wanted to attend another conference without a commons. The commons gave continuity to their experience, their sense of connectedness to themselves and their colleagues, and their excitement about possibilities for healthy cities.

Art teacher Nestor Gonzales, whose students' mandalas and banner designs added so much to the vibrant ambience, came to the commons daily with his family. "For once I was able to come to an event that did not separate me from my wife and little baby," he said. "The commons became my base. People gravitated to me as I carried my baby, and I was able to meet a lot of wonderful people from all over the world."

The Green Oasis Café provided a comfortable atmosphere for conversation. Elementary school children at Walden School transformed recycled containers into vases for the bouquets of flowers that graced the round tables.

The lighted, sparkling six-foot-diameter fountain had a soothing and relaxing impact that may be attributed to the negative ionization that running water generates.

Mandalas made by junior high school students in Oakland enlivened the space.

185

The organizers of a conference for Plutonium-Free Future personalized and enlivened the Veterans' Memorial Auditorium in Berkeley, arranging chairs in a circle and bringing in art and greenery.

Technologies for Creating Instant Commons

To encourage and ease the process of creating instant commons, I identified three approaches, which I shared with my students and others: ENVIRONMENTAL MANAGEMENT, which involves transforming a space by modulating elements in the environment; EOLITHIC CRAFTSMANSHIP, in which potential new uses are recognized in objects that have outlived their original use and been discarded; and QUILTING BEE TECHNOLOGY, based on gathering elements that can without alteration be joined together to form something new.

Environmental Management

The discipline of environmental management was brought to the attention of designers in the mid-1960s by my friend Serge Boutourline, a corporate consultant and pioneer in interactive design. Through it, impersonal institutional spaces can be transformed into welcoming and uplifting meeting places by modulating lighting, temperature, acoustics, seating arrangements, and décor. Simple decoration with posters, banners, plants, and flowers personalizes the space, dramatizing the purpose

The typical classroom with fluorescent lighting and hierarchical seating arrangement fosters passivity and alienation.

or theme of the gathering and creating a supportive setting. Lectures and conferences are enriched and animated by music, poetry, and refreshments that are festively presented. Staging such gatherings as theatrical events heightens the experience for the audience, who should also have opportunities to socialize, meet old friends, and strike up new acquaintances, before and after the event.

Whenever I arrive at a university to give a workshop and lecture, I always analyze the space in which I am to speak. I engage the workshop participants in decorating it with banners and flowers, and, if possible, we modulate the various environmental elements. This transformation of spaces encourages buoyant personal and communal interactions and heightens appreciation of the fleeting precious moments of life. This is particularly dramatic in impersonal institutional environments.

Audience participation in the transformation process provides in-time experiential learning—object lessons that can encourage participants to personalize their immediate surroundings, releasing them from the role of passive spectators. At the beginning of a lecture I encourage an audience to feed back their experience of the lighting, temperature, acoustics, and seating arrangements. To sensitize an audience to the impact of space and the possibilities for improving it, I ask "How can you make yourself more comfortable?" And "What can we do right now?"

When I checked out the hall for a city-wide public lecture sponsored by the Continuing Education Program at the University of Louisville in 1972, I noted unpleasant, glaring fluorescent ceiling lights. To create an alternative, I clamped incandescent lamps onto thirteen tripods around the walls of

In the presence of
candlelight an audience
becomes more relaxed,
receptive, and sociable.

the room. Once the audience filled the lecture hall, I directed their attention to the fluorescent lighting and asked what they thought of it. They expressed their dislike, but also a fatalistic acceptance. When they agreed to participate in an experiment, we turned off the fluorescent lights and turned on the incandescent lamps. The sighs of relief were fully audible. I enjoyed providing this real-time learning experience.

I illustrate most of my public lectures with color slides, so I am particularly dependent on the control of outdoor light and the availability of electrical outlets and extension cords. If light from windows and skylights cannot be blocked, it is futile to attempt a slide presentation during daylight hours.

Moving the chairs in a meeting room into a circle or U-shape so participants can make face-to-face contact is helpful but not always possible as seats in lecture halls are usually immovable and placed in rigid rows. If there are a lot of empty seats in the front, I always ask the audience to come closer so we can make better eye contact. In addition to addressing lighting and seating, I ensure that the sound system functions well, and I adjust the temperature and open or close windows as needed.

Plants and trees in an indoor environment have powerful effects. Not only do they purify the air as they absorb carbon dioxide and produce oxygen, but they also provide subtle energy interactions between plants and people. The simple act of placing one potted plant or a vase of flowers on a table will go a long way toward humanizing an otherwise sterile environment. In addition to creating a more relaxed and inviting ambience, large plants can be used to define the space.

Nurseries will often loan plants for a few

Large plants framed the stage in the Healthy Cities Conference commons.

Volunteers arranged flowers and greenery into centerpieces for tables in the Healthy Cities Conference commons.

Carrying large plants on loan for the occasion into the auditorium for the First International Ecocities Conference in Berkeley

days, particularly when they are acknowledged in an event program and on a sign placed near the plants. It is important to plan a strategy for watering to keep the plants healthy while protecting the floor and surfaces of the event host. A daily misting will help mitigate the effect of insufficient sunlight and fresh air.

Plants can also be used ceremonially or symbolically. For example when I gave talks in February, at the end of a dreary winter, I would often take in bunches of forsythia forced into bloom, since their bright yellow blossoms evoke the coming of spring.

My most memorable experience of instant transformation of space took place in 1981 after I conducted a week-long community design-and-build service workshop with students of landscape architecture at University of Oregon in Eugene. I was scheduled to deliver a final public lecture as the culmination of the week's activities. When the students showed me the lecture room, it looked like an auditorium in a medical college. It was huge, with steep slopes of hundreds of seats, like a mountain side. I had shared with the students my strong conviction that one should ceremonialize and celebrate every occasion, especially when someone travels a long distance to give a lecture. I pointed out that the staging of lecture events provides an opportunity for the host to create a welcoming and fitting ambience that will put the

A deep sense of connectedness is evoked by the act of lighting candles and placing them amidst others or holding or carrying them.

Eolithic Craftsmanship

An *eolith* (*eo*, dawn, earliest; *lithos*, stone) is a relic from the Stone Age, a piece of stone that was picked up and lightly fashioned because its shape seemed suitable for a particular use—as a hammer, a grinding stone, or a spearhead. The eolithic craftsman of today takes advantage of the inherent structure of discarded objects, envisioning new uses, often combining elements to create an altogether new tool or amenity. Economically disadvantaged children work prolifically in eolithic mode, taking full advantage of the structural potential in broken furniture and other discards, creatively refashioning them into delightful, although often unsafe, play equipment. Creating new uses for cable reels, which are often discarded by industry, is a good example of eolithic craftsmanship.

audience at ease and reinforce the presenter's message.

Unbeknownst to me they had seized on the opportunity to put these ideas into practice. Half an hour before the lecture, a group of them approached carrying long bamboo branches. Since it was in May after the rainy season, they also brought rhododendron branches in full bloom. Before I knew it, they had put the bamboo behind the seats and flowers in between. Everyone who came in was given a lighted candle. As I delivered the lecture, I looked upon what seemed to be a hillside glen with many beautiful faces illuminated by the candlelight and surrounded by flowers and plants. It was a moving experience.

[Editor's note: Although fire safety is not addressed in this chapter, it should be integral to design and use of common spaces.]

Gathering materials for building commons

Rolling a cable reel into the Red Barn

Planting unauthorized flowers under the darkness of night

Decorating walls with posters and banners and covering a bare bulb with a paper shade

In the spring of 1973 I conducted a workshop, "Towards a Humane Environment," co-sponsored by the University of Louisville's Allen R. Hite Art Institute and its Center for Continuing Education, with the aim of heightening student understanding of how physical surroundings affect our existence. The program consisted of six lecture/seminars exploring the planning and building of man-made settings that nurture rather than destroy a sense of community. Each lecture began with dialogue among classmates about their classroom environment. They were asked to observe and analyze the space and suggest whatever changes were needed to transform it into a warm, congenial environment.

An old factory building known as The Red Barn had become a student hangout. The students worked together to transform it into a classroom–coffee house, open to the community. They used cable reels to construct tables on which they placed candle holders made of driftwood. They used old whiskey barrels sawed in half to make planters. Candles and flowers on each table imbued the space with a celebratory ambience. The students modulated the harsh light of hanging bulbs by covering them with beautiful multi-colored shades, which they made with paper. For each lecture the students decorated the room and organized a potluck meal. The creation of warm, friendly, humane environments for the lectures inspired people to meet, talk, share ideas on the lectures, and become involved with each other.

After a few lectures we were inspired to green the surrounding outdoor environment by planting flowers surreptitiously under the darkness of night. In an evaluation at the end of the workshop one participant shared her realization that "we can all be designers within our own private environments by using whatever means are available to us, how-

Children enjoyed creating a mural.

Sidewalk Commons at a Louisville, Kentucky fair

Live music animated the Sidewalk Commons.

ever meager, to make our personal environments more livable."

Later that year I heard about an arts-and-crafts fair in which about 400 booths were to display their products but no space would be available for people to meet. I suggested to students from the Allan R. Hite Art Institute at the University of Louisville that we create a "Sidewalk Commons" and offered my lawn and backyard as a staging area. In a day and a half at almost no cost, we created the commons on a small plot of grass, using cable reels from the gas and electric company for tables, borrowing chairs from a funeral home, and defining the space with orange

and yellow chrysanthemums planted in tubs made from half barrels donated by a cooperage firm. Soil and flowers were donated by a local nursery. Students recruited entertainers to provide music and acquired art supplies that children could use to express themselves on large feedback boards. In a few hours, the students built a tower-like structure, easily seen from the street to draw attention to the commons. On the day of the fair young and old came together to rest their feet and enjoy live music. Each student had made a unique contribution to the work. Having shared a vision and a small project, they were no longer strangers to one another. This is an excel-

193

The Cable Café functioned as a commons for Antioch Human Services students.

A typical Saturday potluck lunch

lent example of what I call "building community through environment."

Eolithic craftsmanship was also at play when I worked with students in the Human Services Program in Philadelphia, a satellite of Antioch College where I taught a course in community building and hoped to both foster community among the students and contribute to their growing economic and social self-sufficiency. I also taught a community design-and-build service course that involved students adapting their physical surroundings at the school to better suit their needs. Earlier I had visited Antioch's main campus in Yellow Springs, Ohio, and met with its founder, Arthur Morgan, who innovated "work-study," subsequently adopted by many schools of higher learning. I also talked with one of his sons, a vocal advocate of cooperative grassroots enterprises.

Most of the students were middle- and low-income people of color. Many were homemakers in their fifties and sixties who had received college credit after documenting their past learning experiences. Others were administrators in public and private agencies who used their jobs as a practicum, analyzing how effective they were in their work and how they could advance in their careers.

The school occupied one floor of a high-rise building on a main street in North Philadelphia.

Eolithic craftsmanship inspired the refashioning of these cable reels into shelving and support columns for a Creative Recycling booth at the Boston Flower Show in 1972, a collaborative project I initiated with colleagues, friends, and students from MIT, Massachusetts College of Art, and Harvard.

Since the students were mature working people, most of the learning took place on Saturdays. The neighborhood had only fast food outlets and no grocery stores, so the students had no access to decent food. I suggested that they organize potluck meals for Saturday lunch. We converted one of the rooms into a "Cable Café," constructing tables from old cable reels topped with round pieces of wood, which we covered with red and white tablecloths and vases of flowers.

I helped students produce a newsletter called "Grassroots: the Antioch Community Newsletter." We organized "Green Thumb" workshops to assess their ailing houseplants, and we turned the hallways into a gallery for their work. Since the students had difficulty paying for childcare, we equipped a room to serve as a daycare classroom for students interested in learning about early childhood education.

I also helped them develop cooperative enterprises such as a bookstore that made it easier and cheaper for them to acquire textbooks and other learning materials.

An essential element in quickly creating a functioning commons is finding available waste and adapting it to useful purposes. The creativity and sense of serendipity such discoveries inspire infuses a project with excitement and joy. Cable reels were one of the most useful objects we encountered. At a Creative Recycling Workshop in Boston my students and I also used them to create display shelves. And in Philadelphia's Melon Commons, the first neighborhood commons, we used a cable reel to create a push-go-round, a wildly popular piece of playground equipment.

By the mid-1980s, when I took early retirement from my tenured position at the New Jersey

Hanging the AIDS quilt at the entrance to the commons

Attaching Peace Ribbon segments to create a wall

Institute of Technology to work full-time for peace, I had begun to create instant and temporary commons for conferences and other special events. As an active member of the Nuclear Task Force of the American Orthopsychiatric Association (Ortho), a professional organization that focuses on mental health in the context of social justice, I offered to "ceremonialize" their 1985 Annual Meeting at the New York Hilton. Unlike other associations, most Ortho members work daily directly with disease and social ills. I suggested that the gathering be staged as an uplifting celebration to stimulate healing and creativity and to counteract the misery that abounds in this era of diminishing resources for human services. I would stage a cultural program to dramatize the organization's concerns about mental health and social welfare, and create a commons where people could share their thoughts and feelings. This would enable participants to connect more easily with their inner strength and nurture a sense of community.

My proposal was accepted, and I engaged friends and fellow Ortho members in barnraising the Peace Commons. Henceforth I became Ortho's "ceremonialist," coordinating the creation of a commons at the 1988 gathering at the San Francisco Hilton and the 1989 meeting once again in New York. Others carried on the tradition in 1986 and 1987. Ortho's assistant director, Faith Lamb Parker, wrote to me after the 1986 Annual Meeting in Chicago. "Each year it seems that we understand your philosophy a little bit better."

Quilting Bee Technology

To create the Ortho Peace Commons we used what I call a "quilting bee technology," reusing modular materials, recombining them without altering their form. We designed and decorated a hospitality area using rows of posters on easels and free-standing partitions on which we mounted art displays, photo exhibits, and more.

The Ortho Peace Commons served as a welcoming place to socialize, much appreciated for its decorations, music, and refreshments.

I recruited Phyllis Yampolsky to install her interactive Town Hall Wall in the New York Hilton ballroom. Inside the commons, conference attendees gathered around tables decorated with flowers. Coffee and refreshments were available in a visually pleasing food bar.

For the 1988 and 1989 Peace Commons at the Hilton hotels in San Francisco and in New York, we covered walls with Peace Ribbons, which were loaned to us by the local Peace Ribbon coordinators. The ribbons contained images of plants, birds and animals, children, family, and home. This powerful visual demonstration of people's desire to preserve life in the face of a potential nuclear holocaust created a special ambience of compassion in the commons.

We recruited a yoga teacher for an early morning session and musicians and performers for lunchtime entertainment. We brought in two huge AIDS quilts from the Names Project in San Francisco and used them to frame the entrance to the commons.

For the 1989 Ortho gathering, the Nuclear Task Force proposed a day-long pre-conference institute on "Transforming Spaces into Places for Healing, Community, and Peace," which would culminate in a hands-on, group collaboration of barnraising the Ortho Peace Commons.

197

FOUNDATIONS OF COMMONS BUILDING

For commons building to be successful, several key elements must be present. The following mutually reinforcing components have served as foundations in all commons I have helped to build, from small projects to large sustained ventures.

Start with the People Involved

The design and building of a permanent commons cannot be carried out by outsiders who bring preconceived ideas about what residents want or ought to want. At each stage of the process in brainstorming, in designing, in barnraising, and in animating the finished space—the people who will use the commons must be involved. The community of people eager and willing to contribute to improving the quality of their physical surroundings might include neighborhood residents, women, senior citizens, day care centers, schools, places of worship, settlement houses, and many other grassroots and nonprofit interest groups.

Ask "Who Is Missing?"

Fundamental to the concept of a commons is that no one be left out. At community meetings, it is important to ask: Who is missing? We live in a society that still struggles with racism and discrimination, so we must exert special efforts to assure that we represent a cross-section of the community. If only adults but no youth gather to plan a commons, the community needs to take steps to rectify the situation. Young people are the energy center of a community and can play an essential role in integrating, protecting, and revitalizing neighborhoods. Additionally, in communities where many teenagers have dropped out of school, their engagement in building a neighborhood commons on their own turf can develop their sense of pride and self-worth, as well as marketable career skills.

Recruit Volunteer Professionals

Active citizens eager to participate in construction of public amenities provide a mixed blessing for city governments, as the citizens often lack skill and experience. Volunteer professionals, recruited to work side by side with residents, add rigor to self-help construction projects. Environmental designers, artists, craftspeople, animateurs, social scientists, lawyers, and many others can be engaged, depending on the needs and complexity of the project.

Enlist Organized Volunteer Work Teams

Groups such as AmeriCorps, Scouts, students, religious groups, and nonprofit groups are motivated by a sense of service to their community. In many communities, high school students are required to participate a certain number of hours per year in community service. Unions will support rather than oppose these volunteer efforts because in the long run the heightened quality of the surroundings stimulates the demand for more jobs.

Partner with Existing Nonprofits

Financial aid and administrative support is often available from nonprofit corporations concerned with environmental and social issues. Such organizations welcome the opportunity to sponsor grassroots efforts, and funding for environmental improvement projects, funneled through nonprofit corporations, can come from private foundations, businesses, and governmental agencies.

Get Help from the City

Especially in larger projects, it is possible to partner with city or other public agencies. These agencies may provide funding or the use of heavy construction equipment, such as bulldozers and trucks, to which grassroots communities otherwise would not have access. Public agencies that make resources available for citizen-led efforts demonstrate government in service to the people.

Storage depots can be established throughout the city to make salvageable material easily available. Such depots can make a significant contribution to municipal recycling efforts and prevent the city dumps from overflowing. Municipalities can also establish tool-lending libraries or support community gardens by providing fencing, irrigation installation, and wood for planting beds, along with soil and compost. Citizens and governments in collaboration to improve neighborhoods promote dynamic and mutually respectful relationships with one another.

Use Recycled and Salvaged Building Materials

To keep building costs low, incorporate found objects and salvaged building materials. Every city contains many surprisingly untapped sources of supply. These include donations from businesses, industrial surplus, government and military surplus, and salvaged material, to name a few. A survey can reveal the sources of recycled materials in each local community.

A living city needs the presence of elements from its past in its streets, sidewalks, and public places. "Historic" and "repurposed" local building materials are integral parts of the urban experience and give an air of familiarity to new constructions. They prevent commons from succumbing to a depersonalized aesthetic of mass construction.

Using salvaged materials also gives artists in a community free rein to exercise their skills in improvisational design. Hands displaced by labor-saving technologies are reengaged in a labor-intensive creative process, and dedicated volunteers—many of them highly skilled in the arts, crafts, and trades—have the opportunity, through using recycled materials, to create beautiful yet affordable spaces.

Bringing together resources from various sectors of a city and creatively using inexpensive salvaged materials ensures that commons projects are affordable and manageable.

Putting It All Together

In response to the drastic curtailment of public funding for social and environmental programs during the early 1970s, and to counter discouragement over diminishing resources, I conducted a feasibility study in Louisville, Kentucky, which explored an all-out mobilization of existing physical and human resources for environmental self-help efforts.

The study brought together public and private agencies and residents eager to improve neighborhood environments. For a year I talked with various groups who needed to make improvements in their surroundings and who were willing to work if resources were made available. I also talked with resource groups, such as designers, lawyers, building and plant material suppliers, and representatives of social service and municipal agencies.

The process culminated in an all-day brainstorming forum, where we gathered in "discover and match" sessions to share needs and resources. A perfect match was discovered when a daycare teacher expressed a need for shade trees. "Some days," she complained, "it's too hot to let kids out on that sticky asphalt." A nurseryman quickly offered some overgrown maples he was about to cut down because they were too costly to dig. After a silence, a newly appointed 4-H Club representative for urban programs said, "I often wonder how I can get the kids doing something with nature in the city. I'd be delighted to bring them to the nursery and teach them how to dig, ball, and burlap trees to prepare them for moving." Again a silence. The trees, as all realized, were still a long way from the daycare center. After some thought, a man from the Department of Public Works spoke up. "I have no volunteers and no plants, but if a 4-H team will be at the nursery on Thursday afternoon, I'll have a truck with a winch there to transport the trees to the daycare center." Faces beamed.

Many such collaborations can be generated, for each community contains a wealth of latent human and physical resources. Bringing together resources from various sectors of a city and creatively using inexpensive salvaged materials ensures that commons projects are affordable and manageable for the people involved. The exchange also forges relationships between public and private sectors and brings government agencies into direct accountability with neighborhood residents. Relationships among people from different sectors of a community can be improved and large projects made feasible. When individuals become involved in the ongoing greening, crafting, and aesthetic refinement of their habitats, they develop buoyant relationships with the physical surroundings of their homes and neighborhoods.

Three Levels of Commons Building

Besides cooperative neighborhood commons, people need commons wherever they gather. Impersonal conference hotels, institutional lecture halls, and commercial street fairs can be transformed to create a commons that enhances relaxation and communication. Thus, three levels of commons evolved in our work, according to the needs of the people and the available resources:

Instant Commons

If very limited resources are available and participants will only use the commons for short periods of time, organizers can create an instant commons by adding simple decorations that personalize the surroundings. They can also change lighting and seating arrangements, and animate the space with cultural activities. Such instant transformation enlivens whatever gathering is underway, from a lecture to a conference session. Instant transformations are also lessons in environmental management; they empower and challenge the audience, or inhabitants of spaces, to change their surroundings to suit their needs.

Temporary Commons

With more resources, communities can spend time and energy to change a space. They can create temporary commons with movable stage settings for special occasions, and animate the space with more elaborate cultural and social activities. The temporary commons featured in this book were all created for special events, such as a multiple-day workshop or conference, for which we spent weeks or months in advance, planning and constructing temporary stage settings and programs.

Lasting Commons

When abundant motivation and ample resources exist or can be acquired, a community can create a more lasting neighborhood commons. A comprehensive space might consist of a sitting area, a playground, and a performance space. A network of common spaces interspersed in a community garden offers opportunities for gardeners, their families, and friends to socialize. These small-scale commons become new public amenities that reinforce neighborhood life.

In the early neighborhood commons, where the focus was on construction and planting was minimal, maintenance of the commons became a burden to neighborhood residents. With the passing of time, my focus with neighborhood commons shifted toward community garden commons, in which individual creative expression blossoms in the midst of cooperative effort.

Building Neighborhood Community

A neighborhood is a place where people converge to realize their lives. Our schools, offices, recreation areas, and places of worship often lie outside our neighborhood; we interact with people there only through the roles they play in those particular contexts. By contrast, in a neighborhood, people get to know each other in the multiple roles they play—as neighbors, parents, and partners. In our neighborhoods, we practice the art of living, and engage in the most essential human activities as we raise children and care for and nurture one another.

In our post-industrial society, families often find themselves living an isolated and segregated existence without the emotional and physical support once provided by traditional extended-family living. To nurture the growth of a new kind of extended family based not on blood relations but on growing friendship, mutual aid, and intergenerational support, neighbors can collaborate in planning and constructing an easily accessible commons.

Community garden commons enable neighborhood residents with no access to land to grow healthy food close to home. Groups also assemble in commons to celebrate special occasions and to debate issues that affect their lives. Such small-scale gathering spaces may combine the functions of a sitting area, playground, neighborhood park, community garden, or sanctuary.

Neighborhood commons are different from the centralized town commons of earlier American life. Such commons are typically located downtown, surrounded by government and commercial buildings. In these more formal public open spaces, people are only visitors; they cannot till the land to grow food, and people of lesser means often feel out of place. Centralized commons are under the control neither of the people who use them nor of residents who live nearby. The events that take place there are usually organized by governmental or business groups and often attract masses eager to shop and be entertained.

Neighborhood commons are also different from public playgrounds or parks, which in underserved inner-city neighborhoods are often not easily accessible to women with small children, to the elderly, and to people with special needs. Unlike more remote open spaces such as ball fields, parks, and nature preserves, which accommodate specialized uses, small-scale neighborhood open spaces need to accommodate a wide variety of functions throughout the day, evening hours, and weekends, amid the cycle of seasons. Consequently, the design of neighborhood commons is complex and challenging.

The process of building community begins at the earliest stages of shared envisioning and design of a commons. Once a design has evolved that satisfies the future users of a commons, self-help construction can begin. In order to accomplish heavy construction tasks, men and teenagers must be involved, working together with women and children. In many instances volunteer work teams, such as Scouts, fraternities, AmeriCorps, and members of faith communities can be recruited to help with the heavier work. By participating in the realization of a shared vision, the members of a community experience their interdependence.

Community building does not stop when the work of constructing the commons is complete. Commons management provides a new challenge to neighborhood residents unaccustomed to taking on shared responsibilities. Usually a core group of people take the initiative to maintain and administer the commons, so it is essential to the success of the commons to discover and nurture potential leaders, both those who have administrative ability and those who can inspire others to participate.

The potential for community growth is particularly promising in community garden commons. As gardeners satisfy their personal needs through cultivating their plots, they are more open to assuming communal responsibilities for the overall maintenance and administration of the garden and its commons. Working together, people learn to listen to one another respectfully while resolving conflicts and engaging in consensus decision-making. A subtle social fabric of caring relationships emerges as people bond with one another and share events in the commons that mark significant phases in their lives—retirement parties, weddings, healing circles.

In the wake of increasing vulnerability to violence, community garden commons are being challenged more than ever to meet the demand for human contact. Many people are motivated by a deep craving to come together in these spiritually uplifting sanctuaries—to commune with nature and art, relax and meditate or pray, or to use the commons for sharing experiences, thoughts, and feelings.

Since the flow of creativity depends on trust, autonomy, and initiative, it is not surprising that many individual planting beds are truly works of art, inspired by fellow gardeners' support and acknowledging one another in their creative expression. In these cared-for community open spaces, which function as an extension of home territory, neighbors meet casually as part of their daily lives, and forge bonds of trust and interdependence.

Strengthening Grassroots Democracy

The inviting settings of neighborhood commons enrich lives, and as in a small village, residents get to know each other well and become tolerant of one another's idiosyncrasies. Workshops, lectures, and information exchanges that take place in neighborhood commons raise political awareness, deepen understanding, and can lead to the establishment of community boards comprised of women, men, and teenagers, all of whom represent the multicultural and economically diverse constituency of the neighborhood. Active participation of grassroots communities in the political process contributes to a decentralizing of society and strengthens true democracy.

Though small in scale, commons can have a multiplier effect as they permeate the fabric of a city. As neighborhood communities are empowered by constructing and using their commons, a foundation for true democracy emerges. Community control of these small-scale neighborhood commons gives residents a place where they can take a stand.

As people realize their shared vision by successfully constructing a commons through cooperative efforts, they are empowered to take on larger issues. The emotional and social satisfaction they experience through face-to-face encounters and shared accomplishment makes them feel less discouraged and overwhelmed by the threatening issues they confront in their daily lives.

Unfortunately, any improvement in the physical environment also raises property values, which leads to gentrification of neighborhoods. The cost of consumer goods and services rises along with the real estate and becomes less affordable to longtime residents, who are often forced to relocate. But as property improvements often include the conversion of derelict vacant lots into attractive neighborhood parks and community gardens, the ability of local residents to grow fresh produce close to home mitigates some of the economic pressures caused by gentrification. Other counter-gentrification strategies, such as affordable housing and accessible public transportation, can help sustain the stability of multicultural and economically diverse neighborhoods.

Staging celebratory events in decentralized neighborhood commons strengthens the cohesion and vitality of a neighborhood and imprints it with festive expression. Although large-scale, multicultural events and celebrations in the downtown

squares of cities encourage citizen participation, talent and resources are usually siphoned out of ethnic neighborhoods, which are not enriched culturally or physically by the event. When citizens can voice their grievances and hopes collectively in neighborhood rituals and celebrations, downtown commons can become a forum for citywide festivities rooted in grassroots democratic participation.

Reclaiming the Commons

At its heart, commitment to building commons rests on the idea that all members of a community have the right to their shared natural habitats of land, water, and air. From time immemorial, people from indigenous land-based cultures have celebrated their sacred relationship with and free access to nature, which has assured their sustenance and survival. Yet throughout history, and especially in the history of the West, people's relationship with nature has been severed and their access to public land severely curtailed through the encroachment of private property. The increasing enclosure of common public land has also limited people's ability to interact cooperatively with one another.

More recently, another enclosure has occurred. Increasingly hazardous car traffic has encircled residential neighborhoods, bringing to an end the vibrant social life that once took place in the streets and on sidewalks, stoops, and porches. Neighborhood streets, which residents once experienced as an extension of home—where they hung out casually to share stories, exchange information, and watch their children play—have degenerated into mere thoroughfares for automobiles.

In some neighborhoods, homeowners replaced their stoops and porches with front lawns or gardens that provide a buffer from the noisy, air-polluting traffic. Fences, hedges, and cars parked in driveways now separate houses from one another and isolate residents from contact with their neighbors. In more crowded neighborhoods filled with apartment houses, the only place children have to play is in the streets amid dangerous traffic. The hazard and noise of traffic and the flow of people rushing by inhibit friendliness as neighbors hesitate to stop on the narrow sidewalks to talk.

Many cities throughout the world have developed speed bumps and curb extensions for slowing down traffic in residential neighborhoods, making the streets safer for bicyclists, pedestrians, and especially for children. Holland and Denmark have created "home zones" in high-density areas that change the function of a street by adding amenities, such as sandpits for small children, basketball hoops, play houses, hopscotch grids, and colorful plantings.

In the United States, urban community gardens are one of the last remnants of the commons. Within them benches, chairs, picnic tables, barbecues, and vine-covered arbors provide comfortable sociability settings. For decades they have infused the fabric of American cities with flourishing vegetation amid sterile buildings and streets, and have provided places where family members, neighbors, and friends cultivate friendship and community.

Unfortunately, today, in neighborhoods across the country, community gardens are threatened. Two dynamic trends in urban development are on a collision course, and the survival of community life on neighborhood blocks is at stake. On one track, a growing number of community gardeners and advocates for healthy and livable cities assert the need for accessible open space in residential neighborhoods. On the other track, city administrators, coping with fiscal crises and eager to take advantage of the demand for land for housing construction, have been selling off city-owned vacant lots once leased to neighborhood residents for community gardens. As these last remnants of public land are sold, neighborhood community is threatened or destroyed.

Creating commons and neighborhood community requires social and political activism to prevent speculative housing, even affordable infill housing, from occupying all available open space in neighborhood blocks. Unless needs for housing and neighborhood open space are balanced, the existence of neighborhood community is in jeopardy. More affluent neighborhoods and gated communities, with fiscal resources and political weight, do have their commons, but these privately owned commons are restricted to the exclusive use of their members. Neighbors elsewhere can stake their claim and secure land for open spaces by introducing guidelines into their city's general plan directing government to secure publicly owned open space, especially in densely populated low-income neighborhoods.

Animating the Commons

Once a commons has been built, it is animated and reanimated through daily use and care of the space, as well as by periodic rituals and celebrations. The root of the word animate is *anima*, or soul. When we participate in celebrations, ceremonies, and rituals, we confirm the importance of our lives and our relationship to others and the world around us. Many of the customs and traditions that once rooted us to our past and gave our lives meaning have disintegrated. People today search for meaning at every level of their existence, in their personal lives, work and spiritual life. We face the challenge of keeping alive for ourselves and future generations the deep satisfaction created by shared, meaningful events. The word companionship holds within it the key: com-pan, "bread with others." Breaking bread together—sharing food and drink—needs to be a vital part of every gathering.

From the beginning, my students, colleagues, and I envisioned neighborhood commons as "ennobling places of meeting where young and old may gather to engage in spontaneous and staged celebrations of public life." Such events range from simple to elaborate—engaging musicians to play during work parties or an open house; creating welcoming settings for meetings and workshops; staging festive dedication ceremonies with music, poetry, and food to celebrate the hard work and generosity of the various contributors; celebrating personal milestones for community members; forming healing circles; hosting performances or exhibitions to showcase the work of local artists and crafts-people. People sense the dynamic energy inherent in the creative process and want to be a part of it.

Ideally every block should have its own neighborhood commons. Margaret Mead wisely suggested that one apartment be reserved for common use in densely populated high-rise buildings to help reduce the alienation and enmity suffered by people cooped up in their own small apartments. In a groundbreaking research project on human development based in Chicago neighborhoods, Dr. Felton Earls of Harvard School of Public Health and his colleagues discovered that the most powerful factor in ridding a neighborhood of crime and violence is "collective efficacy"—neighbors working together for the common good.

The conditioning of our competitive culture has thwarted our deep craving for community. We need an awakening of the spirit of the commons to dissolve the blockages that keep us isolated from one another. Common goals and joyous social and cultural events help us bond deeply with one another. Gradually we become able to reconnect with our instinctive longing for community and bring forth the enthusiasm and commitment required to deal effectively with the inevitable setbacks, disappointments, and conflicts that arise in any cooperative effort. Building and animating commons provides meaning at every level, from personal creativity and social relationships to working with the natural environment. I hope that these stories and images of instant, temporary, and lasting commons will inspire and guide you in your own community-building explorations and efforts.

Neighbors can stake their claim and secure land for open spaces by introducing guidelines into their city's general plan.

EPILOGUE

I first glimpsed Karl Linn in 1959, as I looked down from the second floor into the courtyard of an old brownstone mansion that the City of Philadelphia had given to Heritage House. At that African-American cultural organization I was the volunteer head of the youth chapter. A drop-out from vocational school with course work in carpentry, cabinetmaking, and drafting, I had gone back to Temple University High School at age twenty to earn my high school diploma with the thought of studying architecture. Karl, a short man in his late thirties, was surrounded by a dozen landscape architecture students under an ample locus tree, in a space paved over with concrete, otherwise devoid of vegetation. He was gesturing energetically, directing their attention to the features of the space. I had no way of knowing, in that brief moment, that Karl's ideas, practice, and the force of his personality would shape my life and work, as an architect, urban planner, civil rights worker, and environmental justice activist for

the next forty years.

After our meeting at Heritage House, Karl became a mentor to me, suggesting books to read and introducing me to an astonishing range of artists, writers, and creative professionals. We walked the streets and back alleys of North Philadelphia looking for vacant land that could be reclaimed—I, a tall and lanky young African American and he, a short, intense Jewish refugee with a thick German accent. We talked to kids playing pavement games, street musicians, and people sitting on stoops or on chairs on the sidewalks. Karl taught me to see the potential in empty lots, back alleys, and shady backyards and reinforced my recognition of the destructiveness of large uncaring urban renewal projects.

Karl taught a generation of architects and planners to see beauty and utility in abandoned and underutilized resources of a city. I witnessed this process firsthand when, during our walks, Karl made me aware of the ailanthus trees growing in people's yards. Most landscape architects saw them as weeds because they didn't conform to conventional notions of street trees. As we walked the back alleys, Karl had me and his students make drawings of what we saw. We began to realize that these places were actually quite beautiful. Karl retrieved from the wrecking yard worn marble steps that had belonged to demolished row houses and used them to build neighborhood commons. These reclaimed treasures that had belonged to the neighborhood were part of a community legacy. Karl trained a whole generation of architects and planners to think like that.

Karl's concept of three levels of commons building—instant, temporary, and lasting—is an important contribution to the theory and practice of design technology. Each level is appropriate to the environment and culture it intends to support. Since Karl understood the creation of common spaces as a primarily social process, he tried to ensure that the construction and environmental craft technologies were scaled to the resources, time frames, and human skills available to the community. Karl sought tools, methods, and materials with which residents and nonspecialists could make a vibrant and aesthetically satisfying imprint on their surroundings.

Gradually I came to understand that Karl was not only reinventing the fields of landscape architecture and environmental design to support social justice and world peace. He was also reinventing social movements to incorporate tools of environmental design. In the early 1960s, Karl began to

develop the field of community design—recruiting volunteer architects, planners, and landscape architects to reinforce and expand the services his students were providing to disenfranchised inner-city residents. Unlike the dominant paradigm of real estate development, community design presumes that those most affected by social and environmental problems should be involved in analyzing the issues, exploring strategies, leading meetings, and developing solutions. Participation is an inherent right, not just a means for getting the project done. Karl's community design studios at the University of Pennsylvania built trust and engagement, integrated the experience of nonprofessionals and professionals, strengthened local networks, and increased the capacity of all participants.

In the middle 1960s, with Lyndon Johnson's Model Cities Program and the War on Poverty, the idea of community design service caught on. Universities adopted it as a teaching tool (like internships or providing medical or legal services to low-income populations). The community design-and-build studio was replicated in a number of other universities such as Harvard, MIT, Columbia, Pratt Institute in Brooklyn, and UC Berkeley. Many students who participated in these studios went on to distinguished careers in the field.

Throughout his life and work, Karl kept alive the idea of the commons, even when the idea was completely lost on most people. In modern society most land-use decisions are privatized, which tends to privilege people with more money and resources and marginalize everyone else. In most traditional societies, people have a direct capacity to come together and decide what is needed for the common good—a grazing field for cattle, a pump for water, or whatever. The idea of common assets has begun to reemerge in public consciousness. Most people believe that air and water should be common assets to which everyone has a right. The patenting and commercialization of genetic material has raised questions about the morality of owning and selling life. People wonder whether broadcasting airwaves, long considered a common asset, should be bought and sold. The models Karl created and the strategies he developed for building commons and community in the modern world can strengthen us in our struggle to survive in the twenty-first century.

In the decades since our first encounter, Karl and I collaborated on many projects. After retiring from New Jersey Institute of Technology in 1987 to work full-time for peace, he moved to Berkeley, California, where I was living. We engaged in dialogues and discussions long into the night about the purpose and meaning of our experiences and how we as environmental designers might work to bring about fundamental social change. Our discussions inspired us to co-found the Urban Habitat Program, at Earth Island Institute, one of the first environmental justice programs in the nation and an important forerunner in bringing environmental awareness to multicultural urban communities. Karl also helped me clarify my own life work of adapting the tools of architecture, landscape architecture, urban planning, and design to help African-American communities overcome our long history of disenfranchisement.

Karl Linn was both a mentor and a friend to me. In the 44 years during which I knew him, our friendship grew. Our paths crossed many times since I first caught a glimpse of him in that old mansion on Broad Street in Philadelphia. Each of our many encounters was both a blessing and a learning experience for me. His lifetime of experience in the struggle to keep alive the idea of the commons is a great gift to the next generation of professionals, whose job it will be to rebuild the places we inhabit, to imbue them with hope and meaning. Perhaps most importantly, these stories and inspiring images can be a guide for ordinary people seeking to change the patterns of destruction in the small corners of our everyday lives.

Now, with the threat of species extinctions and global warming hanging over the entire planet, people everywhere are mobilizing to protect life and looking for ways to make a difference. The tools Karl Linn invented to reclaim the commons, as shown in the designs he inspired and the events he transformed, can help ordinary people build community and empower us to take responsibility for the precious places we share. By working together to find and create beauty in our surroundings, we can begin to build foundations for a culture of peace, justice, and celebration of life.

Carl Anthony

University of California Berkeley students from Habitat for Humanity dig trenches in the southern section of School House Creek Common to drain the area under what will become a sandbox and a children's play area.

AFTERWORD

Karl's vision of the world was huge. He cared deeply about community, social needs, youth, diversity and much more. He dedicated his life to peace, grass-roots democracy, and creating commons, through which he demonstrated his belief that beauty and art belong in open spaces.

This book touches on many of these themes. While Karl's work and focus was on inspiring people to build commons, he wanted his aspirations and experiences to aid and inspire life-sustaining projects around the world. However, because he died before completing this book, Karl didn't have a chance to share many of the day-to-day details that I observed over fourteen years of marriage to him. I hope that recounting them now helps to elucidate how he accomplished all that he did.

Whenever Karl started a neighborhood project, he first noted unmet needs. Were safe playgrounds located too far away? Was garden space nonexistent? He sought out neighbors and natural leaders in the community, particularly women and teens, to get their input about needs and to generate solutions and tactics. Inclusiveness was a driving principle, and the reason why he contacted such diverse groups—churches, local social and arts organizations, businesses, and staffs of public and private agencies. Inspired by his commitment to progressive issues, peace, justice, and environmental groups often became involved in projects, either directly or indirectly.

Karl was constantly on the phone, on the street, in meetings at his home or office—all to further community efforts. Frequently he met people for meals or coffee. He was extremely hands-on and cherished the person-to-person contacts he made. People have said that his passion, warmth, and caring inspired their interest and efforts. In meeting and speaking with myriad people, he sought out their ideas and plans, always asking for feedback, help, and resources. He took input seriously and credited each person for his or her efforts. He followed through and stayed in touch. In my mind, much of his success came from encouraging and supporting others to be creative and to have a voice in the design of their lives. In an era of Internet, text messaging, and the like, Karl maintained a very human touch that was key to his success.

As a population, young people and teens were very close to Karl's heart. He created places for them to "hang out" and opportunities for them to train in various skills, get jobs, and volunteer. He always sought their counsel in designing local commons. In the Melon Commons chapter, he noted the displacement of youth when he wrote, "Youth will be responsible in their community only if they have a vital stake in it." Thirty years later, things haven't changed much. I encourage you to study pages 112–115 in the chapter on Neighborhood Commons of the 1960s for reflections on urban open space that remain relevant today.

Karl had great appreciation for community land resources such as the Trust for Public Land. He focused on obtaining secure access to usable open space near housing for the sake of encouraging community and creating places of peace and beauty. In his introduction to the section on Lasting Commons he wrote: "A variety of government programs made derelict vacant lots available for the kinds of projects we envisioned." And in Washington, D.C. (1960s), while introducing the idea of neighborhood commons, he reported, "I initiated a land-bank inventory of potential neighborhood commons sites, selected sponsoring agencies and recommended sites for development. I mobilized social scientists to document and evaluate the program and located volunteer labor, funding, and salvaged or low-cost construction materials."

In designs for commons, he created options for flexibility of use and maximum participation of users. Designs had ecological features such as solar pumps, cob structures, Flowform fountains, and recycled materials. He encouraged artists and craftspeople and often made connections for them in the community that led to commissions.

Another important aspect of Karl's work was the creation of events and celebrations, which he often documented through photography and film. Karl paid a great deal of attention to aesthetics, including music, candles, flowers, food, testimonial boards, and displays.

As in everything, he made decisions collaboratively and in a nonhierarchical manner. Nevertheless, conflicts sometimes arose, and, when they did, Karl took on the role of peacemaker, mediating and helping to resolve troubling issues.

Also important to Karl's philosophy is that one person or a small team should take responsibility for making all the contacts, educating, and following through. As Karl grew older and especially before his death, he made contact lists and created processes for others to continue his work. To this day, many projects flower and flourish without him.

May all those who love community and life-sustaining creations have huge joy and success!

Nicole Milner

Acknowledgments

It's a great honor to have played a significant role in bringing this book to fruition. In the process, I have learned much more than I could have imagined about editing, budgets, gathering materials, and the publishing process. It has been well worth the effort: Bringing Karl's work to a wider audience couldn't come at a better time in our history.

This book would not have been possible in its present form without the outstanding dedication and thorough attention to detail of graphic designer and editor Diana Young. Diana worked with Karl for many years to refine and translate his rich archive of projects into books. She edited Karl's text and then combined it with the images in a preliminary layout. When Karl died, six of the fourteen envisioned chapters were near completion. He had laid out images for the other chapters and written varying amounts of text, which needed to be assembled and added to the layout—sometimes amplified, sometimes drastically reduced. Following the publisher's advice, Diana lowered the page count by about 35 percent and reduced page width by an inch.

Diana also took on the challenge of creating an additional chapter on lessons learned from the neighborhood commons of the 1960s—condensing archival materials and details from nine partially developed, long-abandoned chapters to reveal underlying themes. She received invaluable help from some of Karl's collaborators, who answered questions, read drafts, and offered clarification and corrections: Carl Anthony (New York), Ron Engel and Neil Shadle (Chicago), Terry Barrett (St. Louis), Mark Feinknopf (Columbus), and Troy West (Pittsburgh). She also drew on audio and video archives recorded by Chris Speeth during Karl's trip to the East Coast in 2002 to revisit projects, most notably dialogues with Paul Hogan in Philadelphia and Kent Cooper and Milton Kotler in Washington, D.C.

For the chapter on Berkeley's EcoHouse, Babak Tondre contributed valuable reflections, details, and photographs. Ted Vorster provided photos and descriptions of the planning, design, and construction of the Ohlone Greenway Natural and Cultural History Exhibit. Photographer Peg Skorpinski graciously granted use of photos commissioned by Landscape Architecture magazine. Janeen Antoine's input, after careful reading of the Ohlone Greenway Exhibit draft, deepened the account of the collaborative process that brought forth the exhibit's most essential section, honoring the indigenous occupants of the land, the Ohlone people.

Others who read drafts and offered comments were Greg VanMechelen and David Arkin (Berkeley's EcoHouse), Sanford Gallanter (Pueblo Cities Commons Cluster), Phyllis Yampolsky (feedback boards at events), Shirley Chesney (Bread and Puppet Theater workshop center), Ted Glick (People's Convention), and Len Duhl (Healthy Cities Conference Commons). Deep appreciation goes to George Cohen for his beautiful photo images of the People's Convention.

Architect David Dobereiner, Karl's longtime colleague and friend, scanned and organized Karl's image archives in addition to commenting on the various drafts. He worked with Karl to select and arrange the images for this book, and did miraculous color correction on some problem images.

Leslie Becker, longtime chair of the graphic design program at California College of Arts and Crafts (CCAC), worked closely with Karl and Diana to develop the page design and typographic styles. Pearl Luke, Canadian writer and editor, polished the text before publication.

While assisting in the enormous task of organizing Karl's archive and developing the commons projects in Berkeley, Nicole Becker typed Karl's dictation for this book and others. Her administrative assistance was invaluable. Thanks as well to editor and consultant Nancy Carleton for her sage consulting services. I wish to express thanks and appreciation to the team at New Village Press, namely, to Lynne Elizabeth, Karen Stewart and Eric Broder. They have been a joy to work with.

Special gratitude goes to Joanna Macy for writing the foreword and to Carl Anthony for writing the epilogue. In their unique ways, each was a good friend and a source of inspiration to Karl.

My deepest appreciation to all those who inspired Karl's work and to those who participated in each of the projects described in the book. Many are named here and in the individual chapters, and had Karl lived, I'm certain he would have added many more of you! You know who you are, and I thank you so much. The true acknowledgments are in the work that continues!

Lastly, I offer my heartfelt thanks to Karl himself for his inclusive and generous love, his visionary rootedness, and his great dedication to building community while creating commons.

Nicole Milner

RESOURCES

KARL LINN & PROJECT-RELATED RESOURCES

A Lot in Common
Feature-length video produced by Rick Bacigalupi in 2003 about the creation of the Peralta Gardens. Karl Linn provides ongoing commentary between interviews with Jane Jacobs, Ray Suarez, Paul Hawken and Carl Anthony.
www.alotincommon.com

Berkeley EcoHouse
Illustrated account of the UC Berkeley class project constructing an ecological tool shed on the EcoHouse lot.
www.ne.jp/asahi/homepage/junichi/ecohouse_en.htm
www.ecologycenter.org/ecohouse

Karl Linn Website
A wealth of information about Karl's life and work that encourages others to build community commons and exchange models and resources. Serves those interested in grassroots community revitalization and peacemaking.
www.karllinn.org

Westbrae Commons Community Art Gardens
Tracy Penner's photos of three Berkeley community gardens that Karl Linn helped bring into being.
http://homepage.mac.com/cityfarmer/PhotoAlbum21.html

CIVIC ENGAGEMENT

Alternatives for Community & Environment
Advocates of environmental justice for low income communities in New England.
www.ace-ej.org

American Friends Service Committee
Quaker organization dedicated to peace and justice.
www.afsc.org

American Orthopsychiatric Association
Organization, once chaired by Karl Linn, supporting civic engagement and non-violent communication.
www.amerortho.org

Beloved Communities Initiative
Network of communities informed by the thinking of Dr. Martin Luther King Jr. and committed to the pursuit of justice, radical inclusivity, health and spiritual wholeness.
www.belovedcommunitiesnet.org

Center for Communication & Civic Engagement
Promotes citizen engagement through research, education and web-based network resources.
http://depts.washington.edu/ccce

Center for Democracy and Citizenship
Develops citizenship initiatives around the concept of public work, including an international youth civic education initiative and community learning centers.
www.publicwork.org

Center for Nonviolent Communication
International training & peacemaking organization, created by Marshall B. Rosenberg, provides support for the living of nonviolent communication in community.
www.cnvc.org

Digital Library of the Commons
Online gateway to international literature on the commons. Searchable full-text articles, papers, and dissertations; and the *Comprehensive Bibliography of the Commons*.
http://dlc.dlib.indiana.edu

Grassroots Global Justice
An alliance of U.S.-based grassroots groups organizing to empower the working poor in a local and global context
www.ggjalliance.org

Institute of Policy Studies
Think tank researching sustainability, participatory democracy, human rights, diversity and international law.
www.ips-dc.org

Journal for Civic Commitment
Online journal about civic engagement.
www.mc.maricopa.edu/other/engagement/Journal

Media Access Project
Promotes right to hear & be heard on electronic media.
www.mediaaccess.org

On the Commons
Project of Tomales Bay Institute on public commons and how to justly and sustainably manage resources.
http://onthecommons.org

Poverty & Race Research Action Council
Civil rights policy organization that advocates strategic solutions to inequality in housing, education, and health.
www.prrac.org

Public Conversations Project
Helps communities with fundamental disagreements over divisive issues to develop mutual understanding.
www.publicconversations.org

Raise Your Voice
Campaign to increase college student involvement in public life and make civic engagement central to learning.
www.actionforchange.org

Urban Habitat
Organization co-founded by Carl Anthony and Karl Linn to advance economic, environmental and social justice in low-income communities in the San Francisco area.
http://urbanhabitat.org

COMMUNITY-BASED ARTS

Alternate Roots
Supports the creation of original art that is rooted in a particular community of place, tradition or spirit.
www.alternateroots.org

**Art in the Public Interest
(Community Arts Network)**
Brings the arts together with community and social concerns, furthering the field of community-based arts.
www.apionline.org
www.communityarts.net

Arts and Healing Network
Online resource about the healing potential of art, that includes healing artist pages, community-based projects, books, grants, newsletter, a Forum, links and more.
www.artheals.org

Barefoot Artists
Multifaceted projects that foster community empowerment and indigenous culture. Founded by Lily Yeh.
www.barefootartists.org

Bread and Puppet Theater
One of the oldest nonprofit, self-supporting theatrical companies, championing a street-theater brand of performance art with shows that are political and spectacular.
www.breadandpuppet.org

National Performance Network
Helps artists make work in their own neighborhoods and to cross geographic and cultural divides to increase the traffic of fresh, challenging artistic work.
www.npnweb.org

Village of Arts and Humanities
North Philadelphia neighborhood initiative offering arts-inspired programs in education, land transformation, construction and economic development.
www.villagearts.org

COMMUNITY DESIGN

Architects/Designers/Planners for Social Responsibility
Works for peace, environmental protection, social justice and healthy communities.
www.adpsr.org

Association For Community Design
Network of professionals committed to advancing research, education and best practices in community design, and to providing a national voice on policy.
www.communitydesign.org

Community Building Resource Exchange
Information about innovative community building efforts to revitalize poor neighborhoods.
www.commbuild.org

Design Corps
Organization that provides architectural and planning services to low-income families in rural areas.
www.designcorps.org

Environmental Design Research Association
International, interdisciplinary organization to advance and disseminate behavior and design research about the relationships between people and their environments.
www.edra.org

Natural Learning Initiative
Research and design assistance program helping create outdoor play and learning environments for children and families. Also training, publications and other resources.
www.naturalearning.org

Planners Network
Progressive association of professionals and activists, involved in planning urban and rural areas in a way that promotes change in U.S. political and economic systems.
www.plannersnetwork.org

COMMUNITY SUSTAINABILITY

E. F. Schumacher Society
Teaches social and environmental sustainability by applying the values of human-scale communities and respect for the natural environment to economic issues. Publications on community land trusts, local currencies, microcredit and the commons.
www.schumachersociety.org

Ecocity Builders
Non profit organization founded by Richard Register dedicated to re-shaping cities, towns and villages in order to improve the long term health of humans and natural systems.
www.ecocitybuilders.org

Evergreen
Motivates people to create and sustain healthy, natural outdoor spaces through three core programs: Learning Grounds (schools), Common Grounds (public) and Home Grounds.
www.evergreen.ca/en

City Repair
All-volunteer grassroots organization that educates and inspires people to reclaim their urban spaces to create community-oriented places.
www.cityrepair.org

International Healthy Cities Foundation
Project founded by Len Duhl to provide over 1000 cities with tools, best practices and progress measures for creating sustainable communities.
www.healthycities.org

National Center for Appropriate Technology
Provides information and access to small-scale, local and sustainable solutions to reduce poverty, promote healthy communities and protect natural resources.
www.ncat.org

National Association of Neighborhoods
One of America's oldest organizations of neighborhood coalitions, block clubs and community councils.
www.nanworld.org

PolicyLink
National research and action institute that addresses poverty and develops policies for social equity.
www.policylink.org

Riseup
Project to create democratic alternatives by controlling secure means of communication, Riseup provides online mail, lists and hosting for those working on libratory social change.
www.riseup.net

SmallCommunity
Website resources to increase the number of small, local communities and strengthen those that exist.
www.smallcommunity.org

Sustainable Communities Network
Website to promote the exchange of information about community sustainability in both urban and rural areas, and to increase the visibility of best practices.
www.sustainable.org

Time Dollars Institute
Expanding the local currency movement to reform economic and social systems, policies and practices.
www.timebanks.org

Urban Ecology
Designs neighborhood plans to meet residents' needs in the San Francisco Bay Area, advocates change, and serves as an information resource.
www.urbanecology.org

GARDENS & URBAN AGRICULTURE

American Community Gardening Association
Bi-national nonprofit membership organization that develops resources and conducts educational programs.
www.CommunityGarden.org

The American Horticultural Society
One of the oldest national gardening organizations in the country, established in 1922, providing America's gardeners with gardening and horticultural education.
www.ahs.org

City Farmer's Urban Agriculture Notes
Non-profit society that promotes urban food production, environmental conservation and political horticulture.
www.cityfarmer.org

Community Food Security Coalition
Committees working on issues of food security ranging from anti-poverty efforts to sustainable agriculture.
www.foodsecurity.org

Growing Gardens
Boulder, Colorado, organization that helps neighborhoods start and maintain community gardens.
www.growinggardens.org

Green Guerillas
Cultivates community gardens, sustains grassroots groups, engages youth, paints colorful murals and addresses issues critical to the future of their gardens.
www.greenguerillas.org

RUAF Foundation — Resource Centres on Urban Agriculture and Food Security
Global network focussed on micro-scale city farming programs & resources. Publishes *Urban Agriculture Magazine*.
www.ruaf.org/

Urban Community Gardens
Online directory of the best sites on how to organize and create a community garden.
www.mindspring.com/~communitygardens

GOVERNMENTAL

AmeriCorps
Program of the federal Corporation for National and Community Service to help Americans give back to their communities. Includes AmeriCorps, AmeriCorps VISTA, and AmeriCorps NCCC.
www.americorps.org

Youth Conservation Corps
National Park Service program that works with conservation agencies throughout the country to provide educational and team building skills for young people.
www.nps.gov/youthprograms/ycc.htm

PUBLIC SPACE

Claiming Public Space
International online participatory network for sustainability, public-interest art, architecture and design community.
www.claimingpublicspace.net

OPENspace Research Centre
Offers practical guidance to planners and designers so that outdoor environments are accessible for all people.
www.openspace.eca.ac.uk

Project for Public Spaces
Organization providing technical assistance, training and research to help create and sustain public spaces.
www.pps.org

Trust for Public Land
Nonprofit organization that conserves land as parks, community gardens, historic sites and rural lands, conducting land conservation and legislation projects.
www.tpl.org

YSPACE
International network supporting youth inclusive policies in the design and management of public spaces.
www.yspace.net

INDEX

About the Author

EVVY EISEN

Karl Linn
1923 – 2005

Karl Linn built communities from the bottom up, working alongside citizens of working-class neighborhoods in nine American cities from Boston to Berkeley. A landscape architect, child psychologist, and university professor, Karl pioneered community design centers and community gardening movements across the United States. He is beloved for his vision and leadership in the field of grassroots community building.

Karl was at home wherever he went, thanks in part to his diverse background. He grew up on his mother's fruit tree farm in rural Germany and fled with his family in 1934 to Palestine, where he studied agriculture, started an elementary-school gardening program, and helped create a kibbutz. Karl moved to Switzerland in the 1940s and earned a degree in applied psychology. From there he went on to New York and worked as a child psychologist, co-founding a school for emotionally disturbed children. Eventually Karl returned to horticulture and rose to prominence as a landscape architect for the corporate and cultural elite of the East Coast. Gradually, however, he experienced the wealthy suburbs as "green deserts," devoid of public playgrounds, sidewalks and benches where people could sit and talk.

Beginning in 1959, Karl taught landscape architecture at the University of Pennsylvania. He would take his students into inner-city Philadelphia, where they witnessed the creativity and ingenuity of working-class communities and reciprocated with design services, helping transform derelict vacant lots into community gathering places—the neighborhood commons this book documents. Over the next decade, Karl started (or inspired into being) community design centers in ten cities. He taught at Massachusetts Institute of Technology, New

221

Jersey Institute of Technology, and other colleges and universities. With passion and determination, Karl would recruit volunteer professionals and local teams of volunteers—many remember those 7:00 AM calls! With them, he would acquire reusable building materials from urban renewal demolition sites, build institutional and government support for their projects, and occasionally create temporary commons for conferences and special events.

Committed to a kinder, more compassionate world, Karl co-founded Architects/ Designers/ Planners for Social Responsibility (ADPSR) in 1981. Still vibrant today, ADPSR works for peace, environmental protection, ecological building, social justice and the development of healthy communities. Karl took an early retirement in 1986 to work full time in the anti-nuclear movement. In 1989, with Carl Anthony, he co-founded Urban Habitat, an organization that continues to empower low-income urban communities to advance environmental, economic, and social justice.

Karl spent his last years in the San Francisco Bay Area, spearheading the creation of a cluster of neighborhood commons projects in his northwest Berkeley neighborhood. Even as he was about to pass away, at 81 years old, Karl seemed to be as comfortable as ever, telling a friend, "You know, I'm very excited about the next phase of all this." After he died, hundreds offered tribute, and a local newspaper noted, "For those he left behind, his legacy is their joy."

new village press

The book you are holding was brought to you by New Village Press, the first publisher to serve the emerging field of community building. Communities are the cauldron of cultural development, and the healthiest communities grow from the grassroots. New Village publications focus on creative, citizen-initiated efforts—good news and good tools for social growth.

If you enjoyed *Building Commons and Community* you may like other books we offer:

New Creative Community: The Art of Cultural Development
　by Arlene Goldbard

Works of Heart: Building Village through the Arts
　edited by Lynne Elizabeth and Suzanne Young

Doing Time in the Garden: Life Lessons through Prison Horticulture
　by James Jiler

Beginner's Guide to Community-Based Arts
　by Mat Schwarzman, Keith Knight, Ellen Forney and others

Performing Communities: Grassroots Ensemble Theaters Deeply Rooted in Eight U.S. Communities
　by Robert H. Leonard and Ann Kilkelly, edited by Linda Frye Burnham

Undoing the Silence: Six Tools for Social Change Writing
　by Louise Dunlap

Upcoming titles include:

Art and Upheaval: Artists on the World's Frontlines
　by William Cleveland

Asphalt to Ecosystems: Design Ideas for Ecological Schoolyard Transformation
　by Sharon Danks

New Village Press is a public-benefit enterprise of Architects/Designers/Planners for Social Responsibility **www.adpsr.org**, an educational nonprofit working for peace, environmental protection, social justice and the development of healthy communities.

See what else we publish: **www.newvillagepress.net**